AF470740

LACE HERE NOW

—

EDITED BY AMANDA BRIGGS-GOODE
AND DEBORAH DEAN

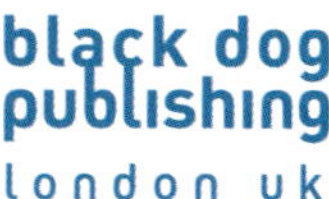

Contents

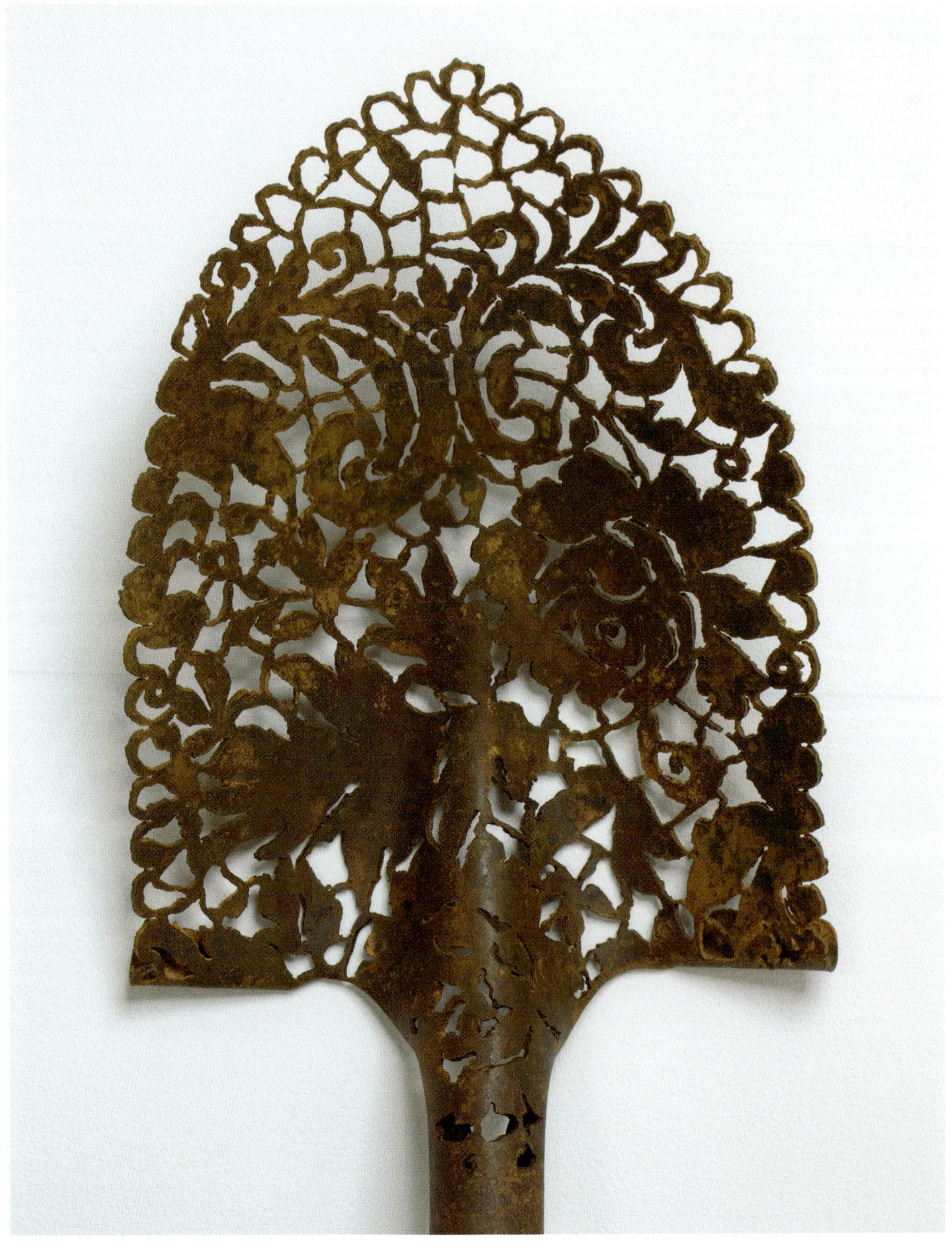

Contents

Introduction

Lace

Here

Now

Cal Lane
<u>Untitled</u>
2006, plasma-cut steel shovel.
Courtesy Art Mûr.

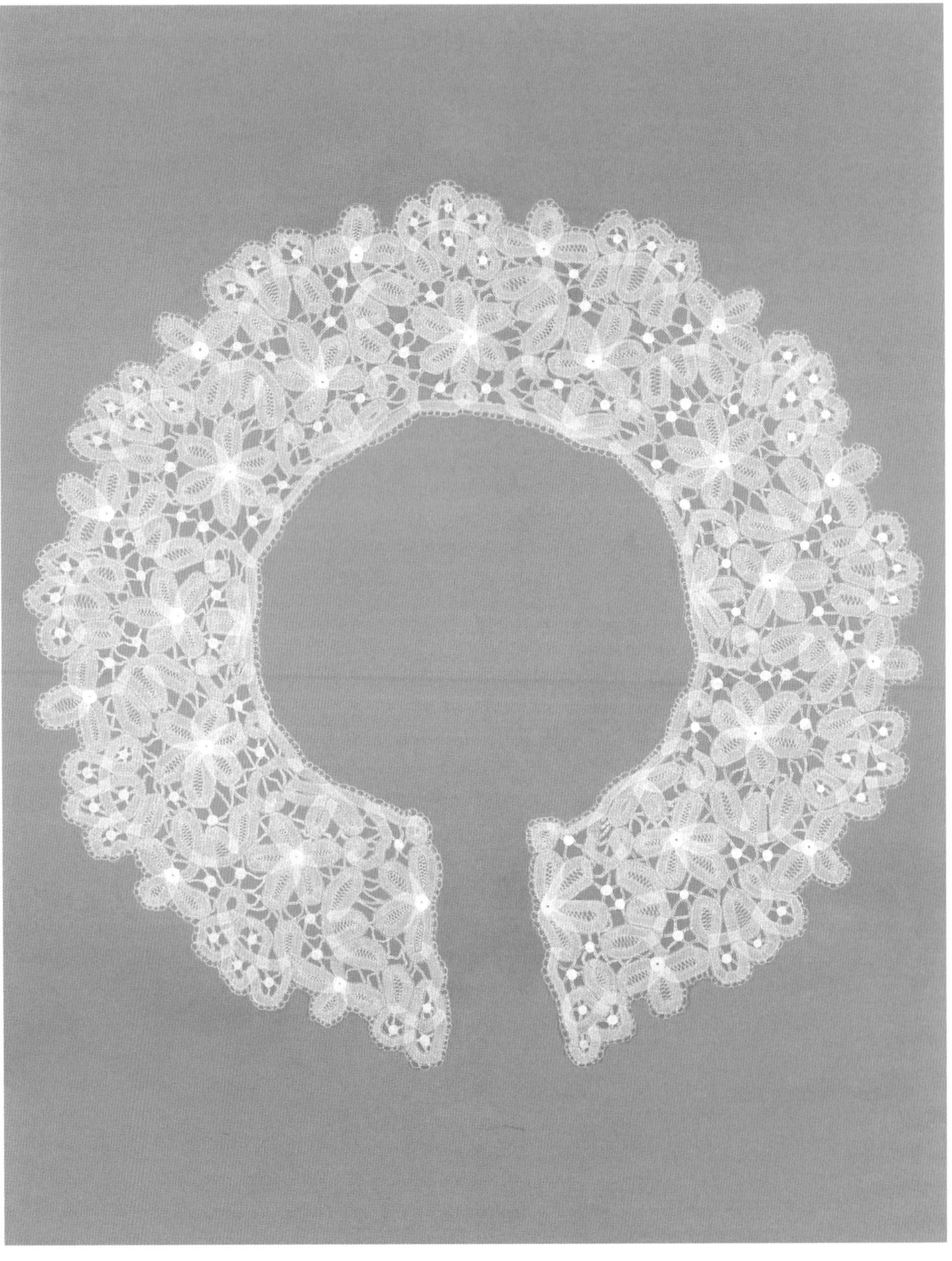

Introduction
Amanda Briggs-Goode
and Deborah Dean

In the autumn/winter of 2012/13 the season of lace related events lace:here:now ran across the city of Nottingham and beyond and brought to fruition a series of talks, collaborations and connections between academics, artists, museums and performers. Initial discussions began in 2008 between Nottingham Trent University (NTU) and Nottingham City Museums and Galleries (NCMG) which led to the emergence of a collaborative PhD project as a potential opportunity to provide some support for the then planned 2012 lace exhibition at NCMG. This appointment provided the catalyst for jointly focussed meetings and research activities which laid the foundation for a wider, Nottingham city-based set of events.

The vision was to celebrate the rich heritage of the once thriving Nottingham lace industry, and to ensure that this inheritance is not forgotten, but is used to fuel and inspire future creative practice. For three centuries, Nottingham was considered to be the centre of lace manufacturing and design in the world and this legacy is still evident within its built environment. The architectural proof of this commercial textile activity is present in the Lace Market area of the city, from the mills and warehouses, to 'Lacey Street'. The recent addition in 2009, of the Nottingham Contemporary art gallery captures the hold that lace had on this area. This is achieved through the building's concrete lace embossed panels, recreated from a lace sample found buried in a time capsule under a foundation stone in the city.

Lace has become increasingly significant within contemporary design collections. A continued interest in the use of lace and reinterpretations of lace patterns was evident in current creative practice, expressing an appetite for an event that focusses on this decorative fabric. A peer review of both NTU and NCMG lace collections early in 2012, also emphasised the regional, national and international significance of lace located within the city. Lace, depending on who and where you are, connotes a myriad of meanings and values—from the 'prim and proper' to its diametric

Teresa Whitfield
Circular Tape Lace Collar
2008, a highly detailed life-size ink drawing of an antique tape-lace collar, 70 x 70 cm.
Teresa Whitfield personal collection.

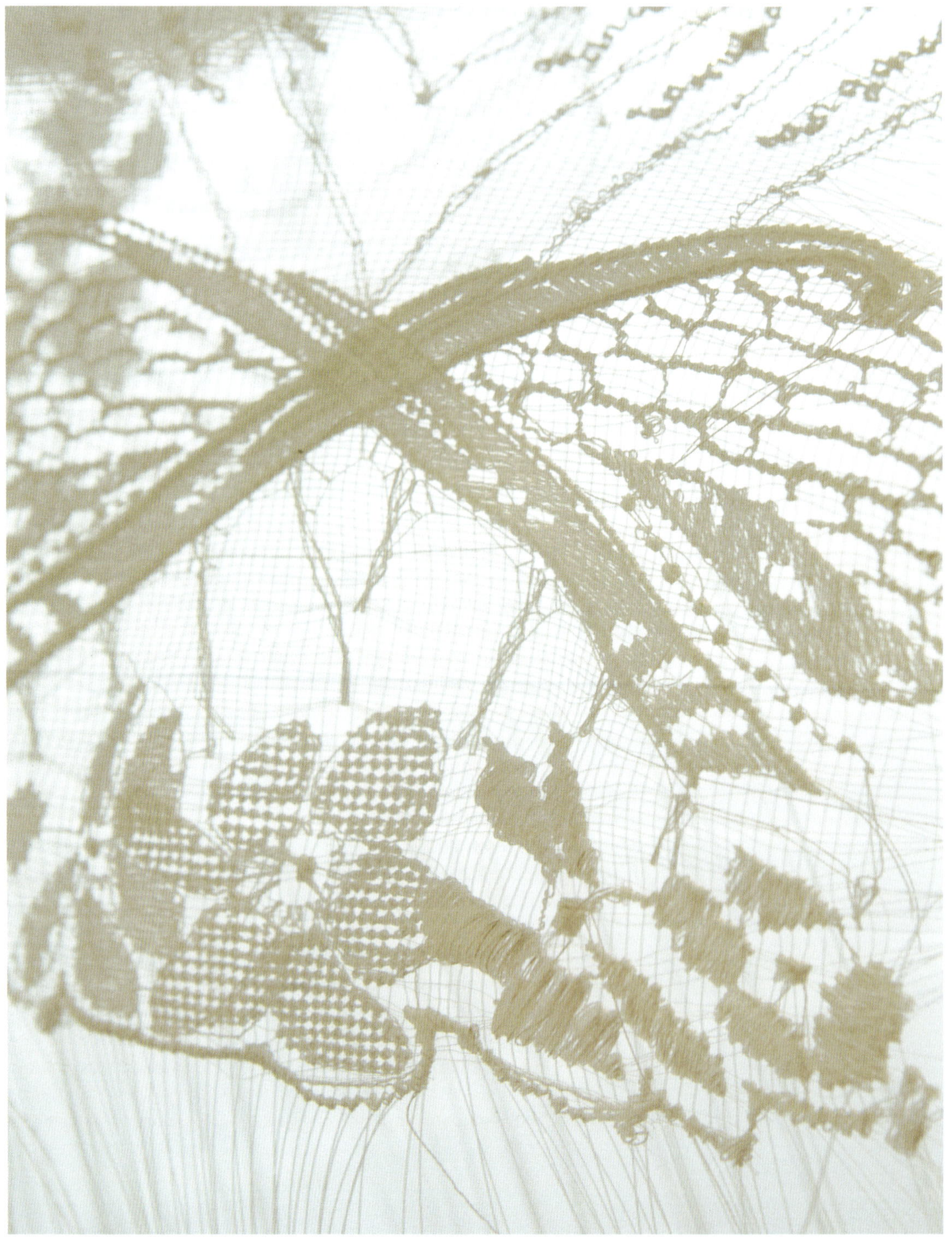

polar opposite—it can be white and concealing or red and revealing as well as cover all manner of meanings inbetween. In this book, however, we wanted to show that historic lace is far from being limited by perceptions and stereotypes and can act as a catalyst for new ideas that challenge traditional definitions of what constitutes this unique phenomenon.

The book is divided into three parts. The first section "Lace" begins with a poem crafted by Deborah Tyler Bennett, which is based upon a photograph found within the NTU Archive from the Walker lace factory. Sheila Mason, a respected authority on Nottingham lace, then sets the scene with her essay about the history of the city's machine lace followed by a visual essay, by Joy Buttress and Matthew Gill, charting the urban and visual history of lace in the city.

In the following section "Here", Judith Edgar talks about the origins and development of NCMG's outstanding collection of lace and lace machinery. This is followed by Amanda Briggs-Goode's essay, which outlines the history and rationale for NTU's important Lace Archive and discusses some of the 'treasures' held there.

The final section "Now" looks in detail at the two exhibitions, which were at the core of the lace: here: now season: Amanda Briggs-Goode's assessment of Journeys in Lace—Parts One and Two curated by Briggs-Goode and Buttress (at Bonington Gallery, NTU and the Wallner Gallery, Lakeside) and Deborah Dean's account of Lace Works the exhibition she curated at Nottingham Castle Museum & Art Gallery. This chapter is given additional depth and scope by the first-hand experience of an artist Teresa Whitfield and her fascination with both machine and hand-made lace, followed by Timorous Beasties' description of how lace has influenced their design practice, and by Cecilia Heffer, who as a designer working with lace archives from Australia, offers a different dimension to the case studies and demonstrates the international reach of Nottingham lace around the globe.

lace:here:now reminds us that lace and Nottingham are unequivocally entwined and that lace still fuels fascination and inspires contemporary art and design practice in the city and beyond.

Postscript: The success of the season was more than we dared hope for. We were delighted by the breadth of interest in the range of events from the press and the public. Regional, national and international visitors descended on Nottingham to enjoy the diverse celebration of all aspects of lace. It was critical in our planning and evaluation of the season to gauge the level of interest in Nottingham lace and the potential for future development. As this was clearly demonstrated we are now conceiving lace:here:now Two.

Tessa Acti
Lace Bird
Embroidery thread, nylon mesh fabric, digital embroidery, 200 x 70 cm.

LACE

Homage to Walker's Workers 1932

It passed through calloused hands, delicacy free-
falling. Embroidered wool, mosaic in imitation lily,
wide-mouthed peony, moss, beaded-vermicelli's
lugworm casts.

Sometimes, its handling a kind of love,
knowing shining-girls never saw the graphite,
pre-bleached state an intimacy between lace
and handler.

Next seen on magazine or mannequin,
all graft rinsed-out, this just the way of it….

Come that photograph, workers' stolid forms
knee-to-dimpled-knee, scrubbed, smiling,
women with pinned-back bobs,
male sea of moustaches, brilliantine.
Most ladies featuring Mum's Auntie Doris,
nod to fashion in court-heeled shoes,
but all in flowered pinnies,
un art-moderne as brick walls…
and not a bit of lace in sight.

Deborah Tyler-Bennett

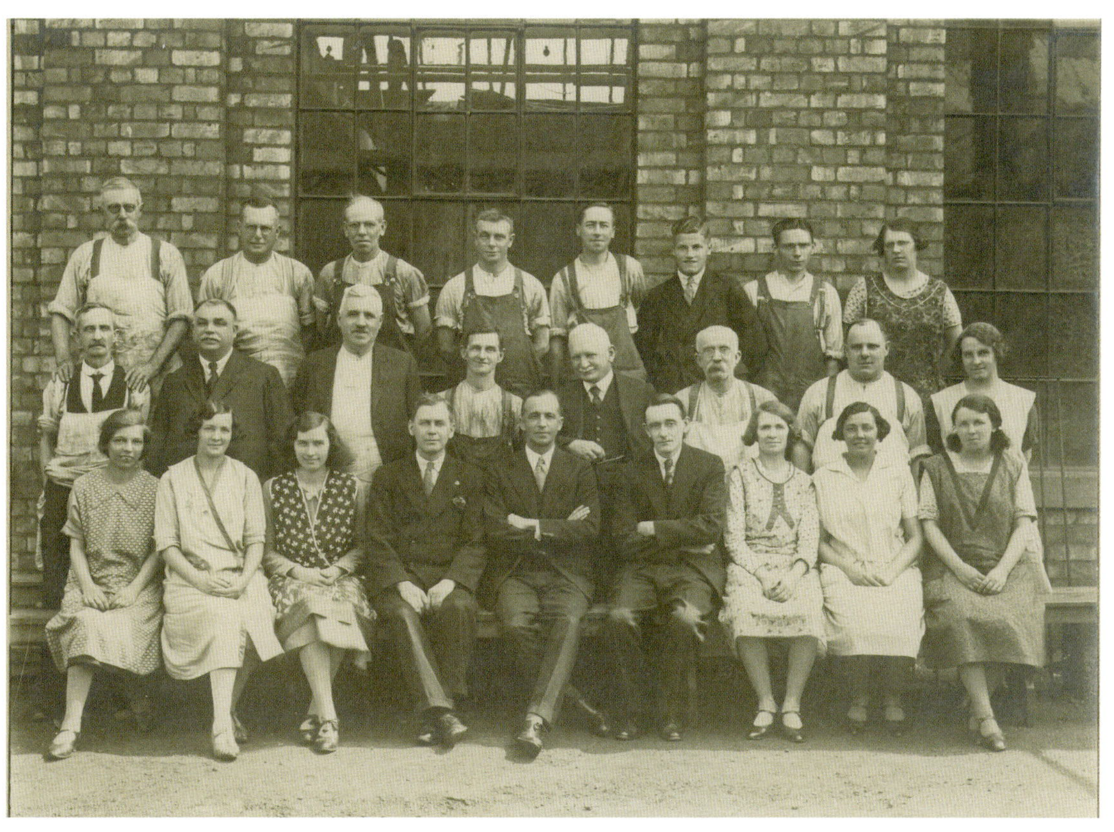

WJ Walker & Son Ltd, 1932.
Courtesy the Nottingham Trent
University Lace Archive.

The Machine-Made Lace Industry Of Nottingham

Sheila Mason

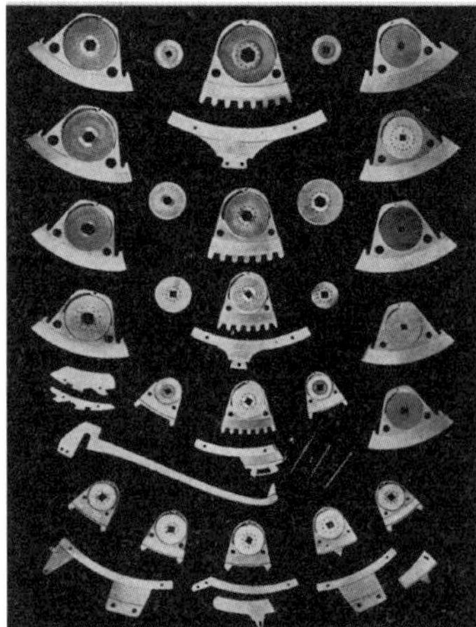

Gamble & Sons Ltd, Twist Lace
Machines Insides Sales Card, 1952.
Courtesy the Nottingham Mason
Collection.

Lace made by machine has been prominent among the industries of Nottingham since the 1760s when net was first made on the stocking frame. It was called Nottingham Lace to distinguish what was then considered an inferior machine knitted lace, with a selvedge on which a pattern was run in by hand, from the integrally patterned hand-made laces. Since then any lace made on the machine has been called Nottingham Lace. Even though most of the actual fabric was not made in Nottingham itself, its manufacture gave rise to a global industry centred on the town.

The machine-made lace industry was not a homogenous entity but a complex web of individual, though interrelated, businesses divided primarily by the type of machine used in knitted and twisted laces, and then divided further by the type of operation carried out in each firm.

The first machine-made lace was knitted from a single thread on the knitting frame. Other than a few patterns achieved by laborious mechanical alterations to the working parts of the machine most of what was known as "point net" left the frame unembellished; patterning was achieved through the work of up to 75,000 hand embroiderers. Point net was knitted until 1820s by which time it had been superseded by knitted warp lace, in which the loop of the knitting frame is united with the warp of the weaver's loom. Warp lace was prominent until the 1850s and then featured little in the machine-made lace industry until the 1950s' introduction of an improved Raschel warp lace.

The second type of machine-made lace is that in which threads are twisted together to make lace in the same way as the hand lacemakers. The first machine of this type was invented by John Heathcoat in Loughborough, Leicestershire in 1808 and was followed by a plethora of different types of twist machines, the most important to the machine-made lace industry being the Leavers machine of 1813 and the curtain lace machine of 1846, both of which were invented in Nottingham. These

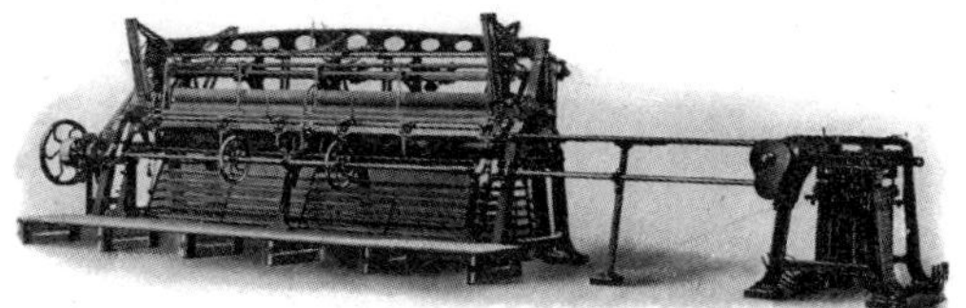

three machines divided twist lacemaking into three sections. The first one was plain net, produced on machines based on Heathcoat's principle, and, after the attachment of the jacquard apparatus between the 1830s and 1850s made the universal patterning of lace on the machine possible. The second and third ones were Leavers lace for garments, made on Leavers machines, and curtain lace for home furnishings, made on lace curtain machines.

After being divided by the type of lace made, the lace industry was further segregated by the various trades in each lace section. Firstly into lacemaking, which is self-explanatory; then into lace manufacturing which encompassed the finishing and marketing of each type of lace, not its making as is the usual meaning of this word, and into lace dyeing, which although closely allied to lace manufacturing was a separate and specialised industry; and finally, into lace machine building and its numerous subsections. The lace industry was composed mainly of a multitude of small firms, often in rented property. However, there were also a few large firms, which naturally became the most prominent. Businesses that combined more than one section were the exception

Leavers Go Through Lace Machine, Nottingham Chamber of Commerce Year Book, 1920. Courtesy the Nottingham Mason Collection.

and usually participants in one section had little or no knowledge of another one.

Nottingham was never large enough, even after the 1845 Enclosure Award allowed expansion into the open fields, or after 1877 when its boundaries were extended to incorporate the surrounding industrial villages, to house the whole of an enormous and diverse industry that continued to expand for 150 plus years and at its peak in the early 1900s employed in excess of 60,000 people, and thousands of machines. Although there were a number of factories in which Leavers lace was made in Nottingham's former industrial villages, most notably Radford, Basford and Lenton, the largest percentage was in the towns and villages to the west of Nottingham, mainly along the Erewash Valley. There was a large firm of plain net makers in Derby but the main centre of production for plain net was in the west of England, in the area around Tiverton where Heathcoat moved his machines in 1816. While from the 1870s the main centre of curtain lace production was the Darvel Valley in Scotland, although there continued to be a few plants of curtain machines in and around Nottingham.

Net and lace from all these centres was processed through Nottingham by the lace manufacturers, who arranged for the transformation of the large webs of, often dirty, unfinished lace from the machines into the clean finished lace required by the end user.

The area of Nottingham still known as "The Lace Market" housed the lace manufacturers, while the dye works and bleaching fields were mainly along the river Leen. Under the control of the lace manufacturer a web of unfinished lace was transported from its maker's factory to one of the specialist lace dye works. After scouring, to remove the 'black lead' (graphite) with which most lace machines were lubricated, the lace was bleached and dyed, the wet web of lace was then stretched on huge frames so that the pattern dried into its correct shape and size. Only when it had been finished was the web despatched to the lace manufacturer's warehouse where it was subjected, by a mostly female labour force, to the myriad other processes still necessary to convert it into the bands, all-overs and curtains required by customers. Tasks such as inspection, mending, and jennying, (in which the separated bands were wound onto cards), were carried out in the warehouses, while other work such as drawing, (in which the lace was separated into single bands), clipping, (in which surplus threads were cut away), and scalloping, (in which surplus fabric was cut away to reveal the curved edge), were carried out by an army of outworkers in their own homes.

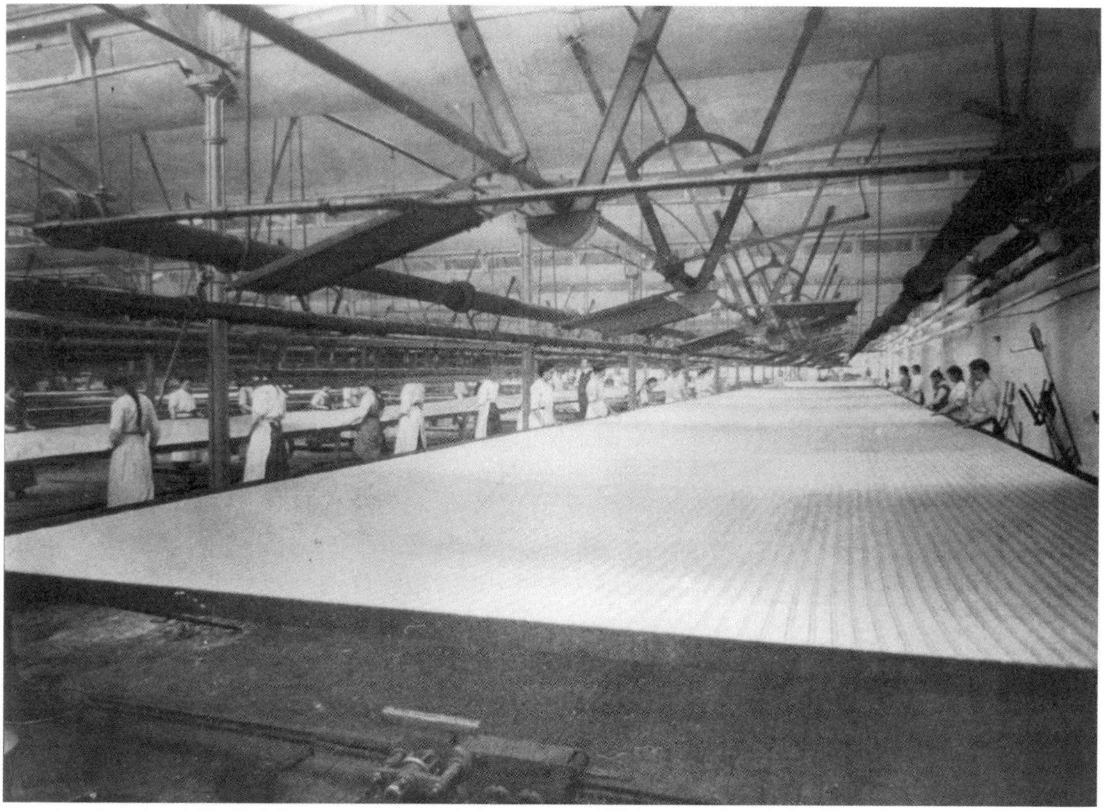

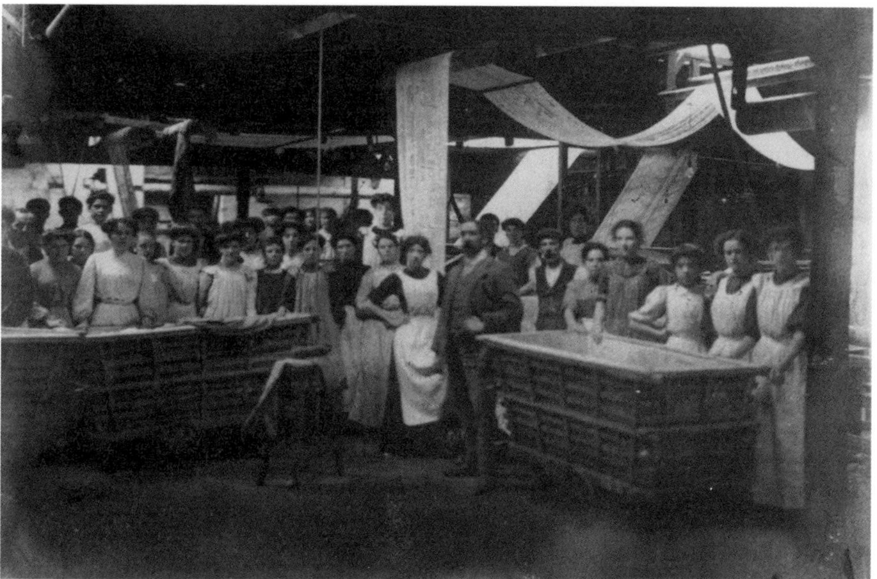

1

2

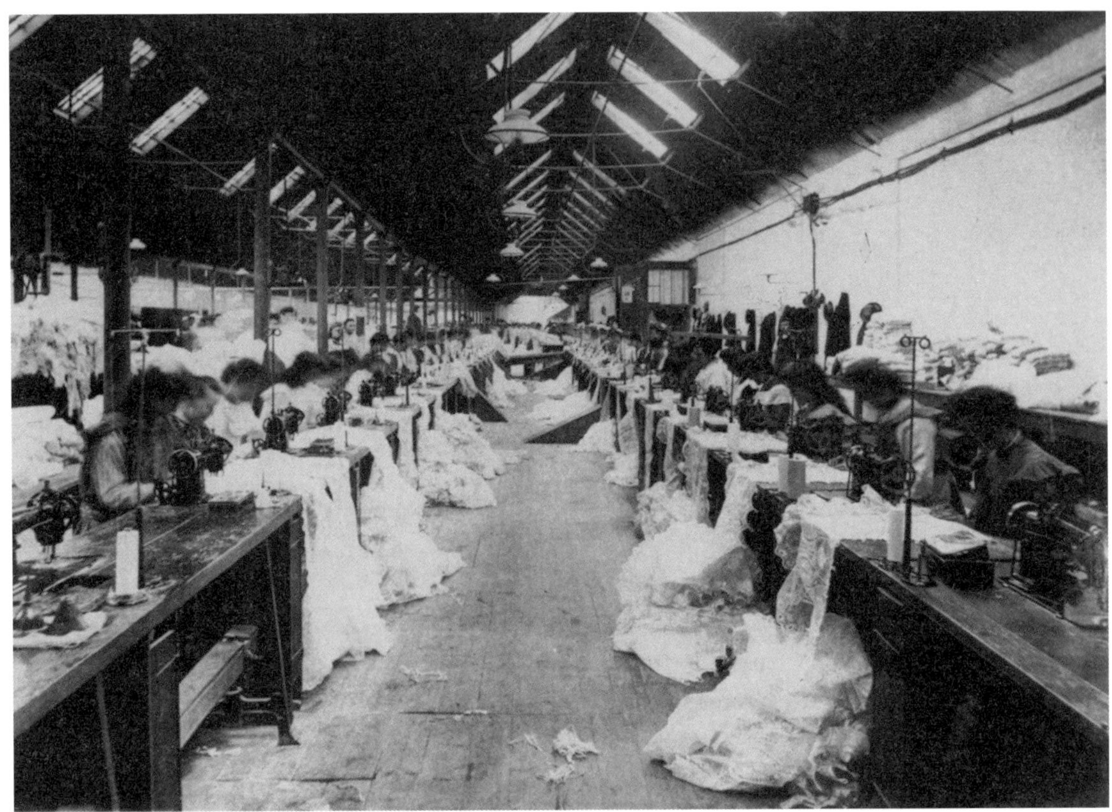

Greater Nottingham was also the world centre of lace machine building. From the beginning of the lace industry until the 1950s more than 90 per cent of the lace machines used anywhere in the world were made in workshops and foundries based in and around Nottingham. A large number of specialist firms made the insides (the working parts) of the various types of lace machines and these were assembled by the builders of the iron machine carcasses into the various gauges and types of lace machines required.

In addition, Nottingham was responsible for formal education for the lace industry. From the time that the jacquard began to be used lace design and draughting were taught. Classes in drawing and design started in 1838 at the Mechanics Institute under Benjamin Heald, who was later to win a medal at the 1851 Great Exhibition for a lace flounce. Then in 1843 the Nottingham Government School of Design opened at

Auxiliary Work at Carey & Sons.
Courtesy the Nottingham Mason
Collection (John Harlow).

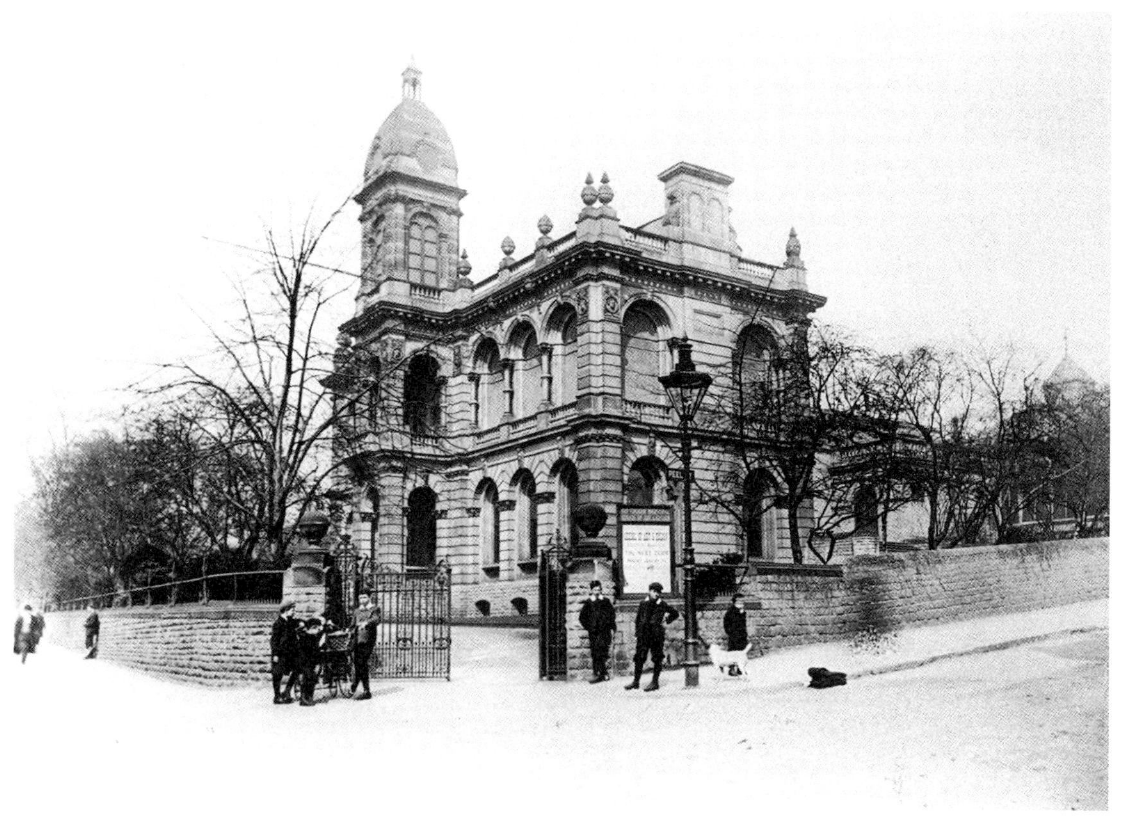

Waverley Building, Nottingham
Trent University, 1843.

the People's Hall in Beck Street (now Heathcoat Street). The school
moved several times, until in 1865 the Nottingham School of Art was
opened; two years after its foundation stone had been laid by the
Duke of Newcastle.

Between 1866 and 1888 the majority of the committee running the
college were lace manufacturers. Initially design was based on samples
of hand-made lace; later folders of printed designs were purchased
from other textile centres. Even then the governors were not always
satisfied that enough attention was being paid to Nottingham's premier
industry as there was only one teacher of lace design on the staff.
However, as there were both day and evening classes the many lace
designers serving apprenticeships in the lacemaking firms were able
to attend; the college continued these lace classes into the twentieth
century. Nottingham Trent University's (NTU) Lace Archive was started

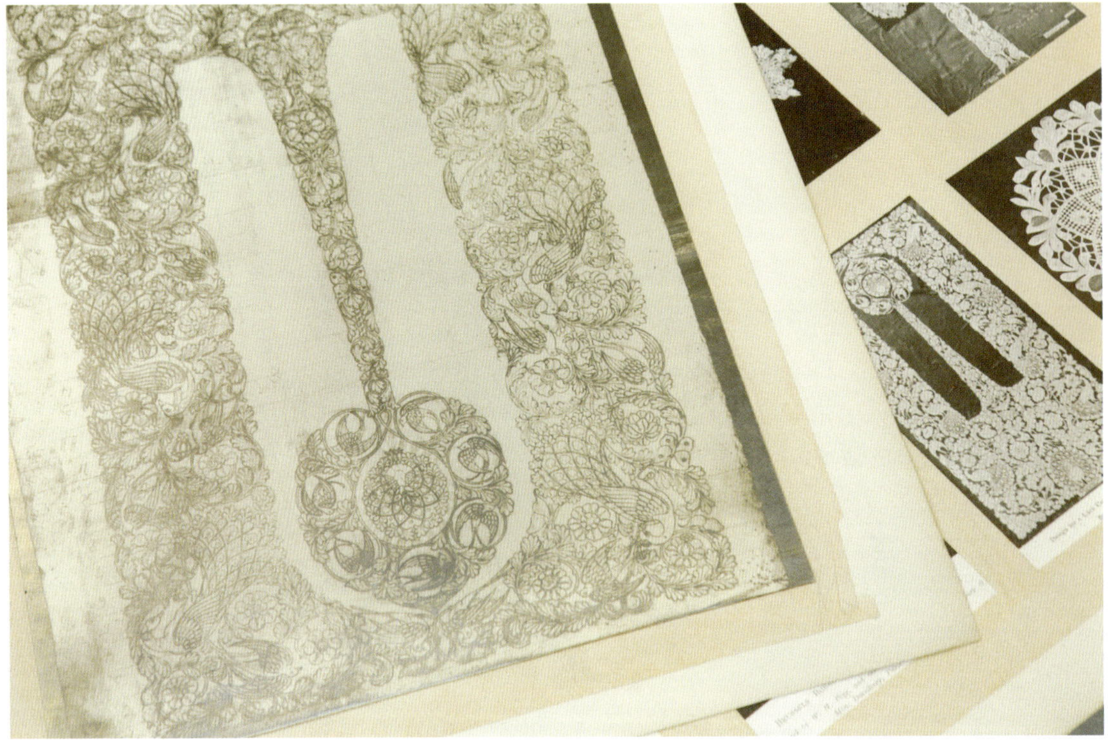

when William Felkin, the 1867 author of *History of the Machine-Wrought Hosiery and Lace Manufactures*, presented the School of Art with four pattern books containing thousands of cotton and silk point laces dating from the early 1800s. In 1909 Jean Senlis, in his thesis for Lille University, *De L'Industrie des Tulles et Dentelles à Calais*, referred to more than 1,500 lace pieces grouped in a museum in the School of Art when exhorting the French machine-made lace industry to establish such a resource.

From the late 1920s a continuing slump in the lace industry inhibited further improvements in its formal education until the end of the Second World War. The College of Art and the College of Technology (which had only started technical education for the lace and embroidery trades in March 1915) still remained independent of each other, although there were joint lace classes in which the lace mechanics learnt design techniques and the designers and draughtsmen the workings of a lace machine. In the College of Art, lace design and draughting classes recommenced, while in the College of Technology instruction in the lace curtain branch

William Pegg, lace curtain design, early-twentieth century. Courtesy the Nottingham Trent University Lace Archive.

was reestablished by 1945, although Leavers machine classes did not start again until the 1950s. In both colleges there were day release and evening classes for lace which at their peak totalled 120 students. In addition to the two colleges, a School for Textiles was started in 1944 for 13 to 17 year olds and those studying lace visited the College of Technology once or twice a week to be taught on its lace machines.

This renewed interested in lace design led to the augmentation of the Lace Archive of the College of Art through the presentation of three collections. The British Lace Federation gave a £250 endowment for the cost of cataloguing and housing the existing lace collection and a further collection of lace and drafts, including those of Pegg. Then in 1944 the lace manufacturer Thomas Adams presented between 30 and 40 printed books about lace and also the pattern books belonging to HB Sketchley, a former director of the company. One book, dating from 1845 and belonging to Zachariah Sketchley, contained laces over 150 years old. In addition, FR Price gave, in memory of his father, GW Price, a collection of outstanding examples of lace draughtsmanship and technique; each sample carried the name of its maker. The Lace Archive of NTU is now the most extensive and important depository of British machine-made lace.

However, from the early 1950s the twist lace machines had to compete increasingly with the improved Raschel warp lace machines imported from Germany. The technical textile department still operated but, importantly, it included conversion courses for twisthands changing over from twist machines to Raschel machines. The College of Art in the 1960–61 sessions continued to offer courses in lace designing and draughting for the Leavers and lace curtain machines, as well special courses for lace warehousemen, but demand for such training was not maintained. After lace instruction in the College of Technology was closed down, the lace machines were moved to the College of Art. There they were used purely for design as classes for the lace trade were reduced to two and totalled only six hours a week.

Of a once great industry employing thousands little now remains. Although the Victorian warehouses still stand and the Lace Market area of Nottingham is an iconic conservation area only a minimum of industrial activity can now be found there. There are no curtain lace or plain net makers, lace manufacturers, or machine builders remaining in the East Midlands and most former lace factories house other occupations. One firm of Leavers lacemakers, the Cluny Lace Company Limited, continues in Derbyshire. Ancestors of the Mason family, its owners, were framework

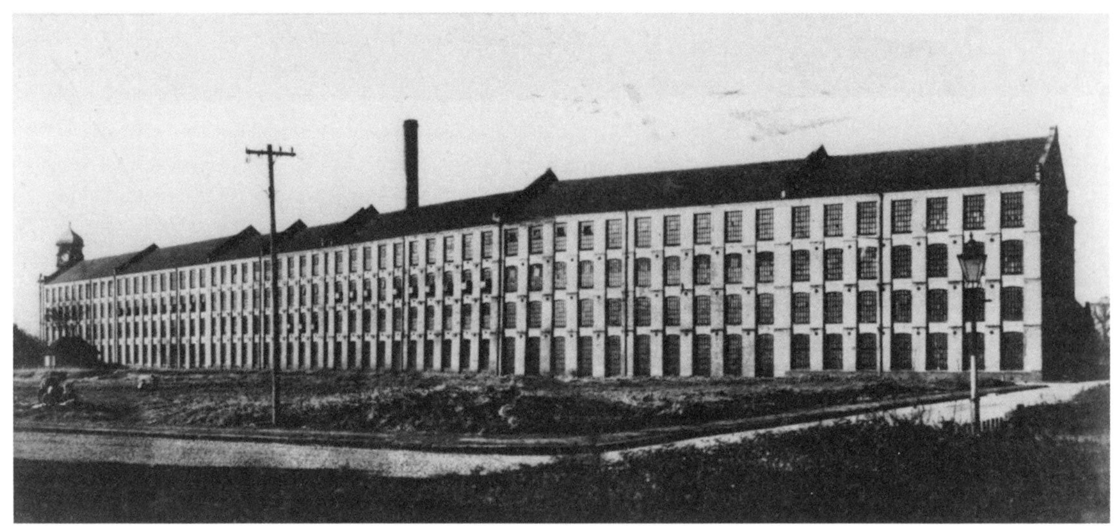

knitters before 1739 and both warp lace and Leavers lacemakers continuously since the beginning of the lace industry. Since the 1970s, as the lace manufacturers closed down, Cluny has carried out all processes in the manufacture of lace, from yarn twisting to dyeing, finishing and marketing. The firm still designs and draughts new laces, and also has a very large database of patterns. Its fine Leavers laces and torchon Cluny patterns can be found worldwide on a wide range of garments.

Victoria Mill, Draycott,
Derbyshire, the largest lace
factory in the UK built between
1888 and 1907.
Courtesy the Mason Collection
(Stanley Wallis).

Nottingham Lace: A Visual Essay

Joy Buttress and Matt Gill

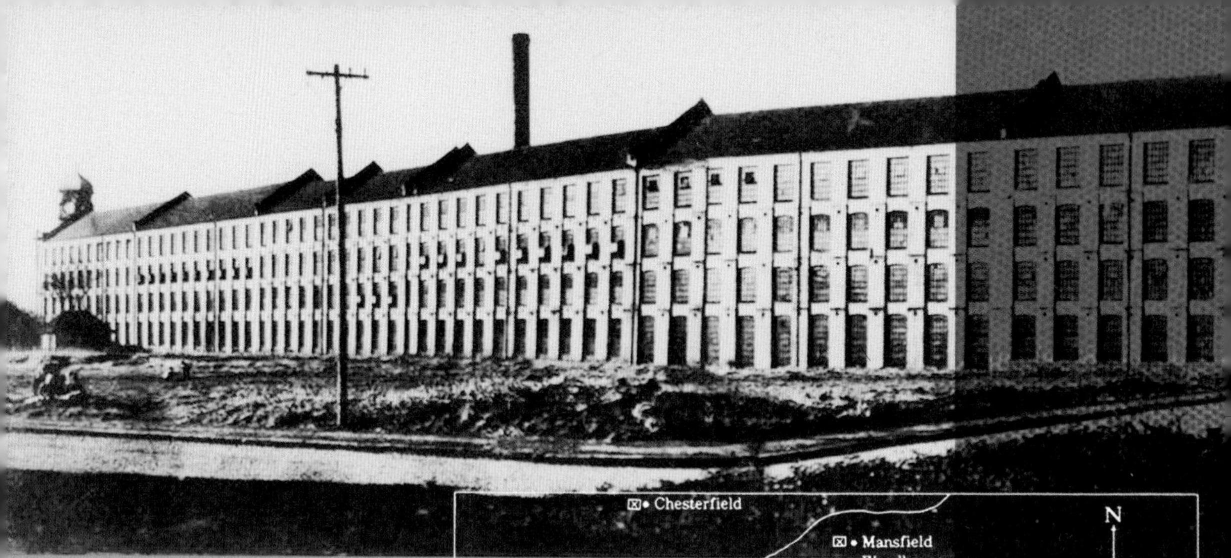

1

1 Victoria Mill, Draycott, Derbyshire.
Sheila Mason Collection.

2 Sheila Mason and Henry Hurt,
<u>Known Locations of Lace Machines
from the 1770s to 1850s in
Derbyshire, Leicestershire &
Nottinghamshire</u>.

3 Adams Building on Stoney St,
designed by TC Hine for Adam,
Page & Co, 1854-1855 and 1865.

4 Birkins Design Room, Palm Street,
New Basford, Nottingham on the
visit of King George V, 1914.

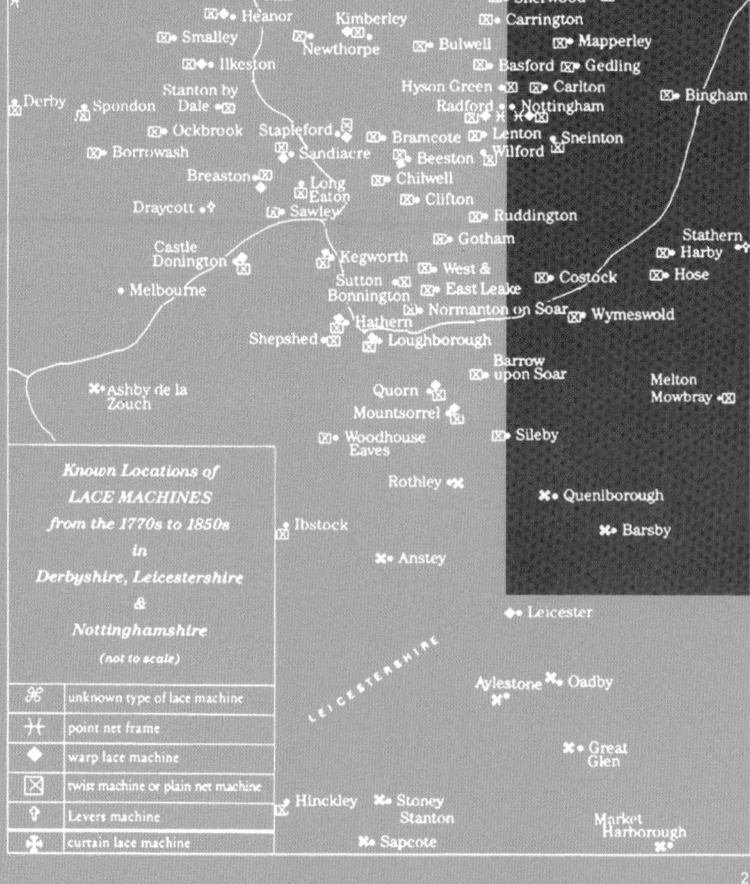

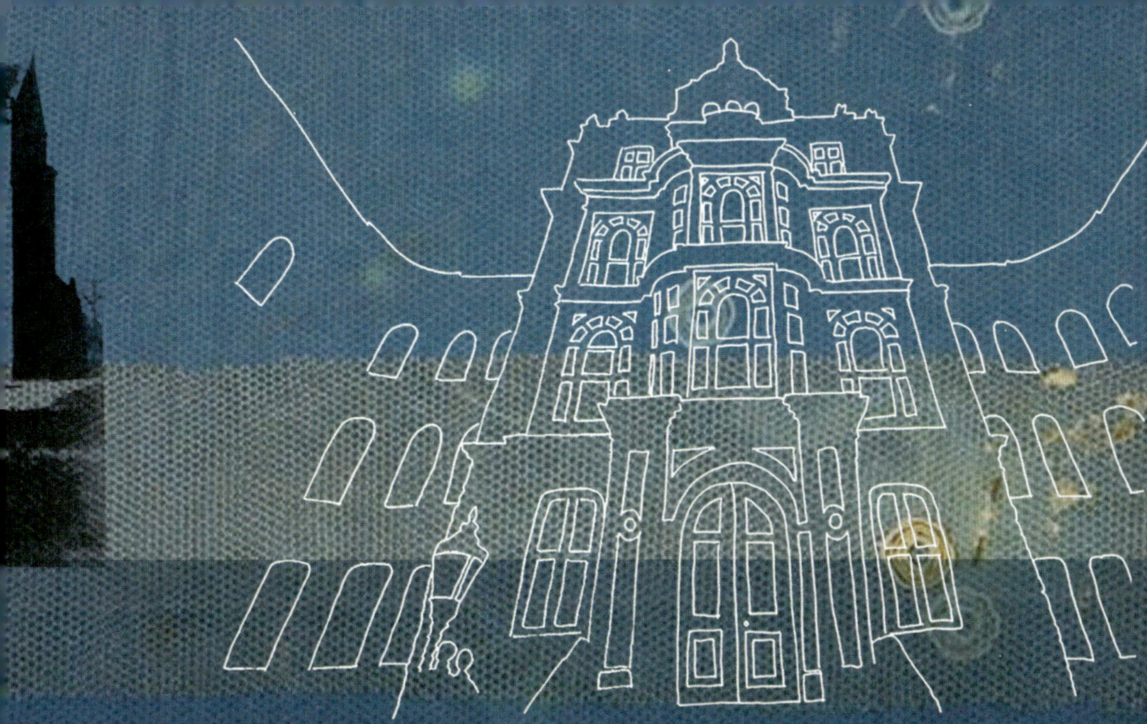

3

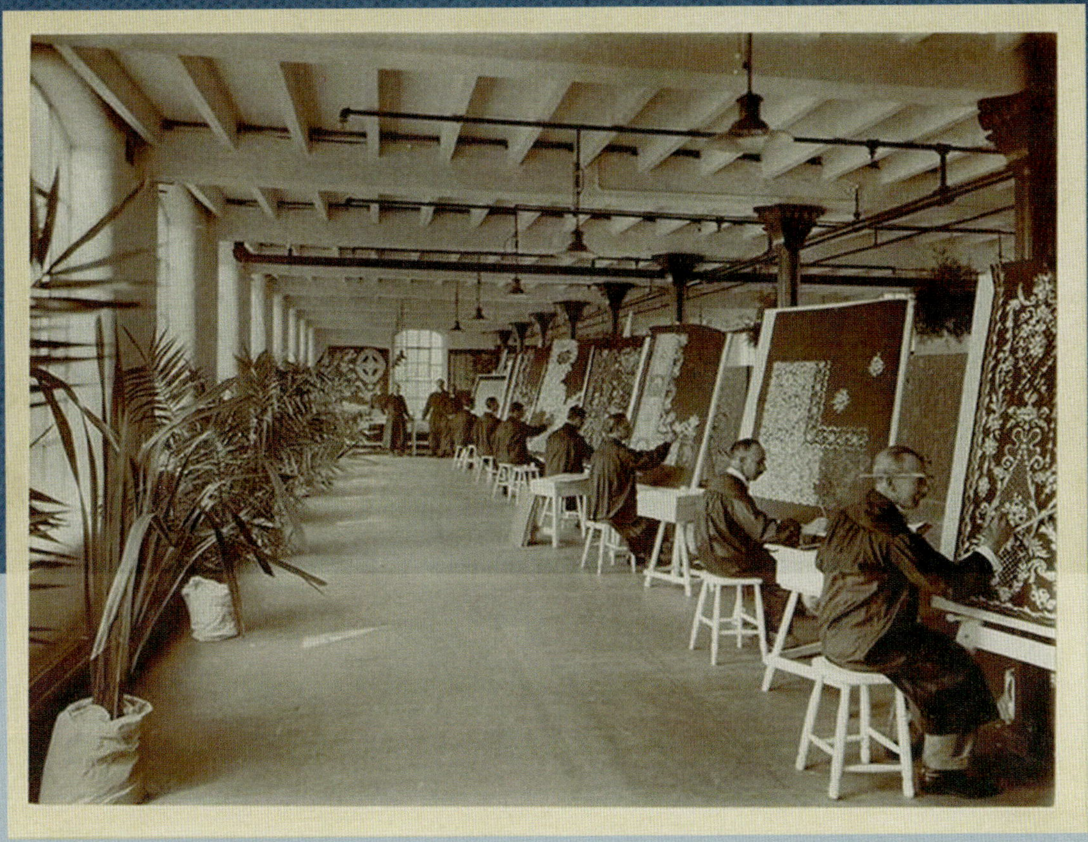

4

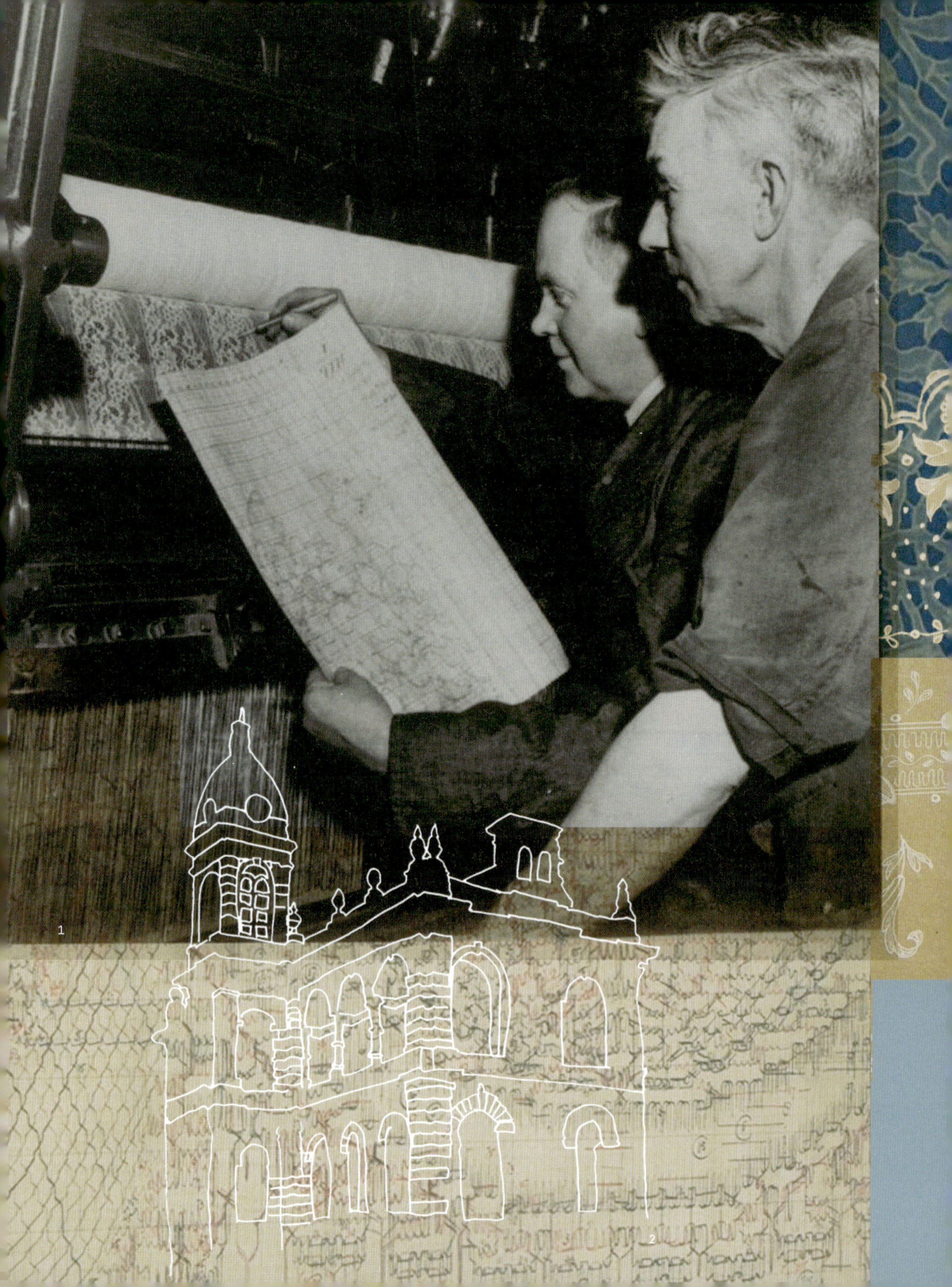

1

2

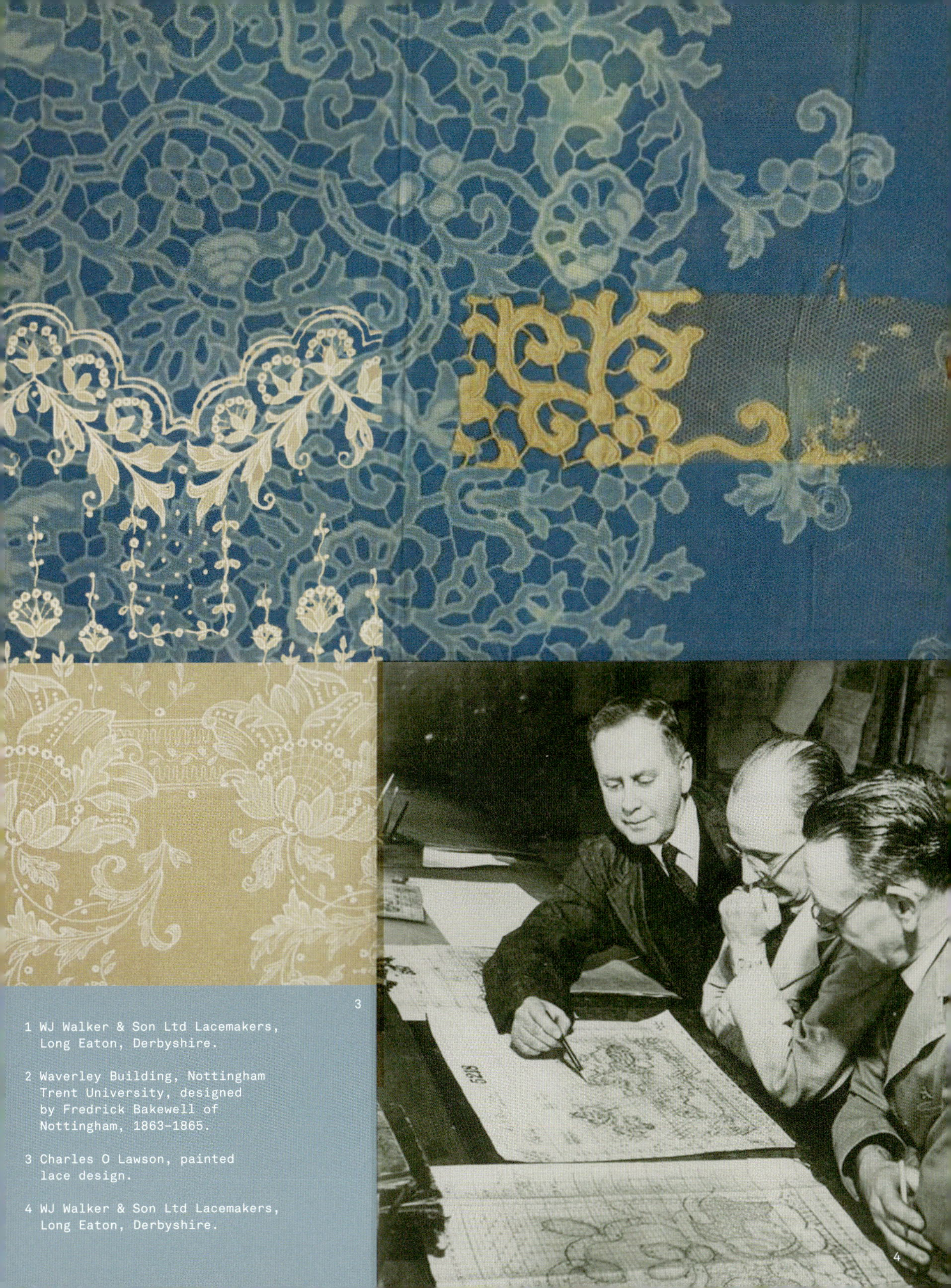

1 WJ Walker & Son Ltd Lacemakers,
Long Eaton, Derbyshire.

2 Waverley Building, Nottingham
Trent University, designed
by Fredrick Bakewell of
Nottingham, 1863-1865.

3 Charles O Lawson, painted
lace design.

4 WJ Walker & Son Ltd Lacemakers,
Long Eaton, Derbyshire.

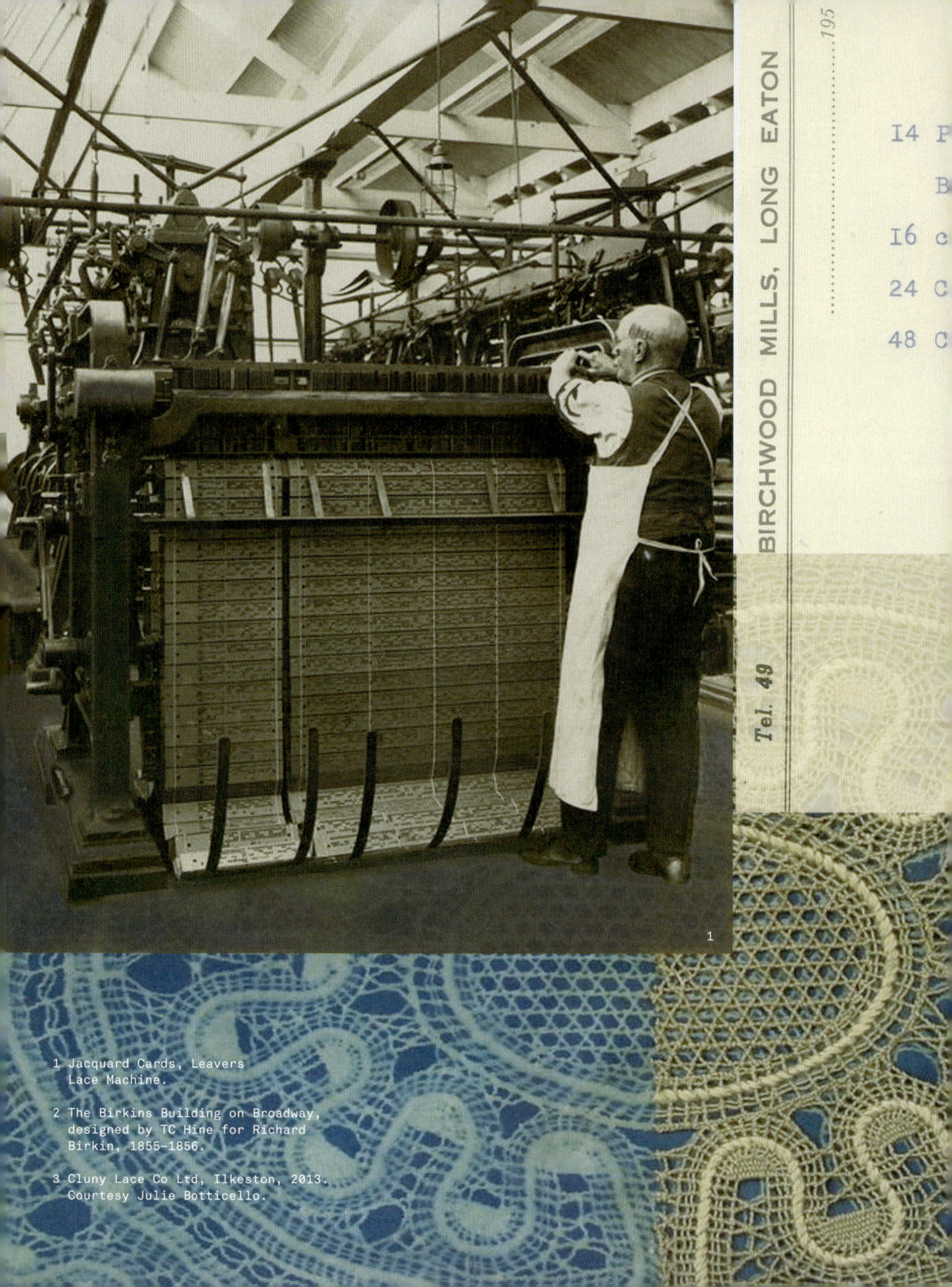

1 Jacquard Cards, Leavers
  Lace Machine.

2 The Birkins Building on Broadway,
  designed by TC Hine for Richard
  Birkin, 1855-1856.

3 Cluny Lace Co Ltd, Ilkeston, 2013.
  Courtesy Julie Botticello.

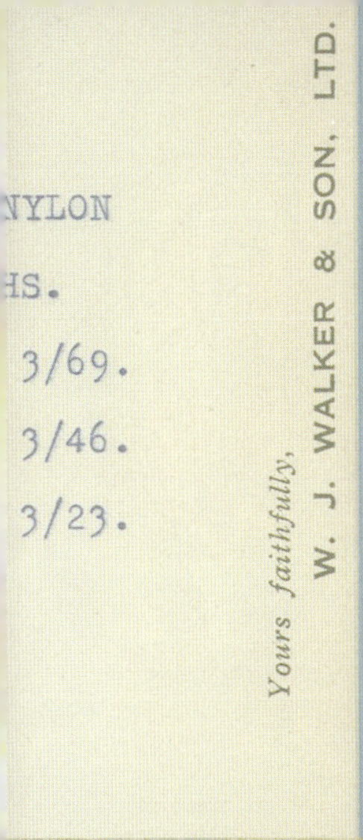

NYLON

HS.

3/69.

3/46.

3/23.

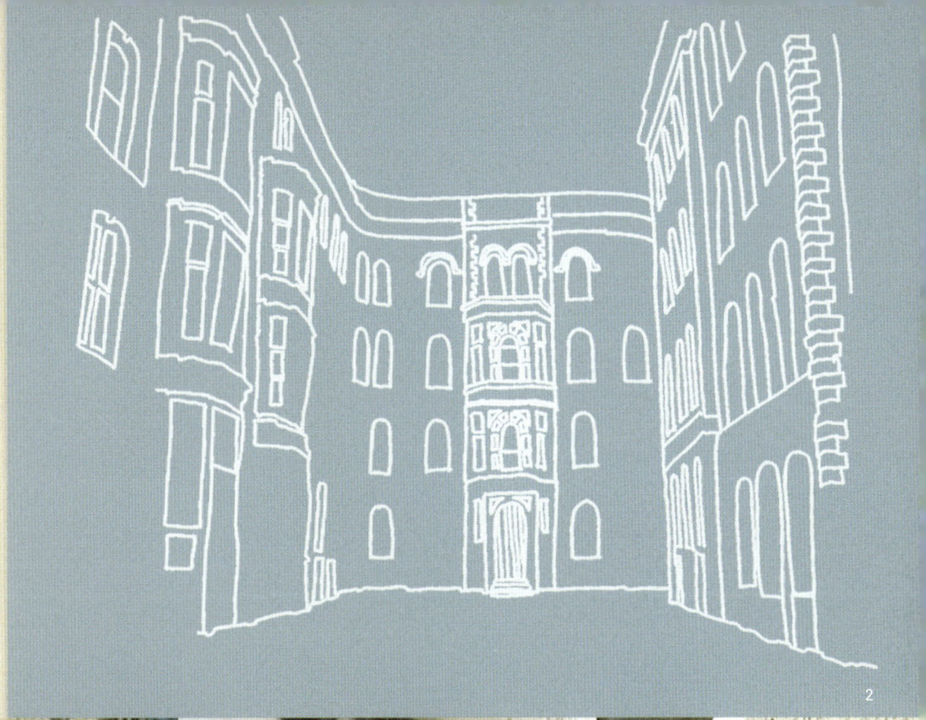

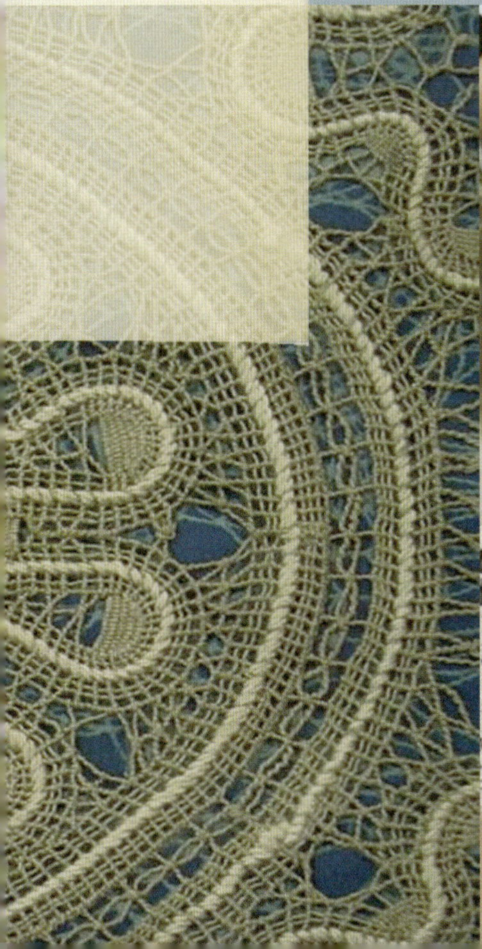

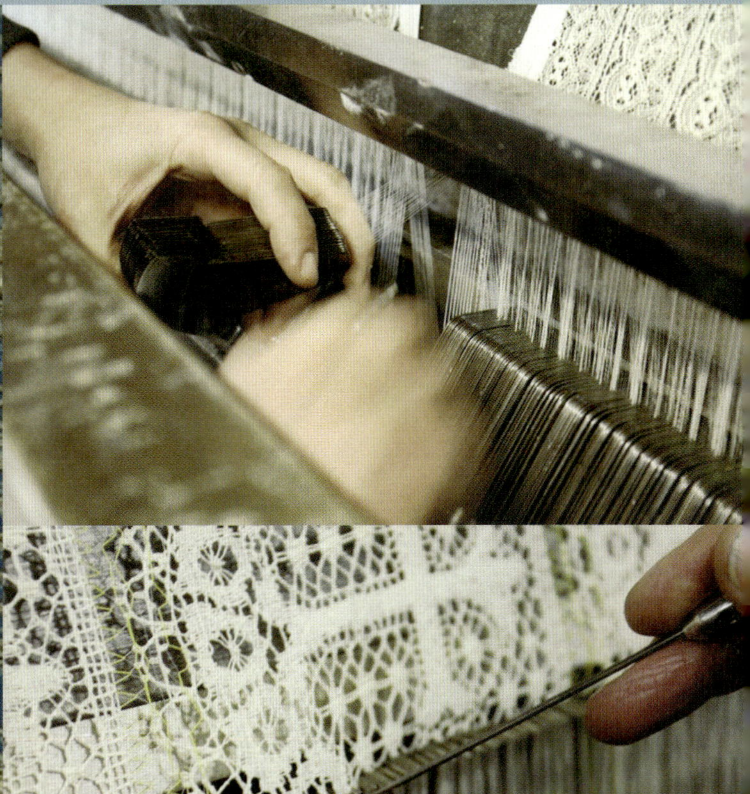

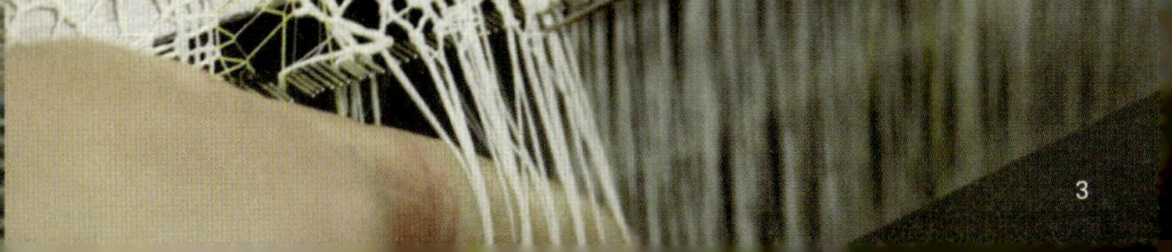

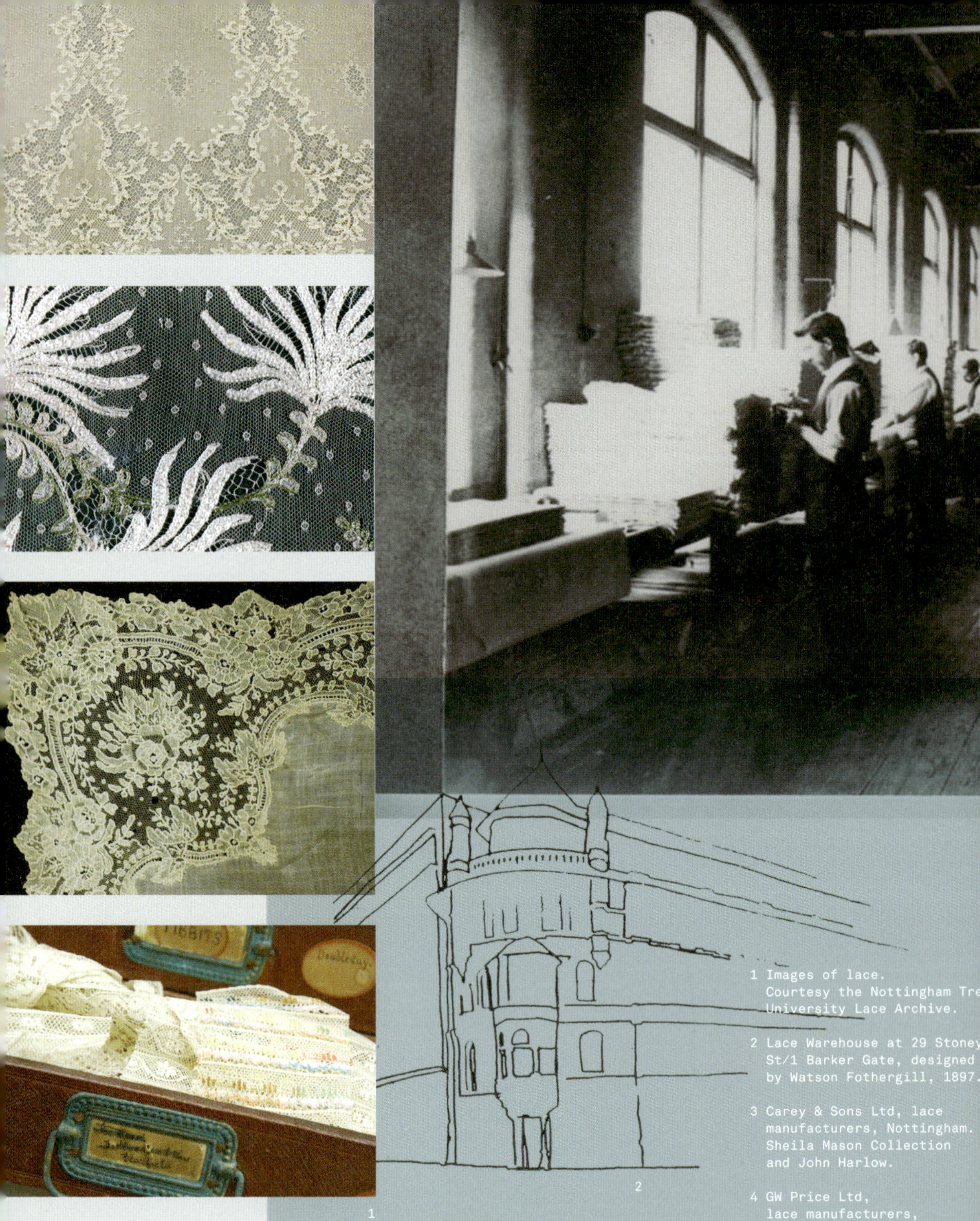

1 Images of lace.
Courtesy the Nottingham Trent
University Lace Archive.

2 Lace Warehouse at 29 Stoney
St/1 Barker Gate, designed
by Watson Fothergill, 1897.

3 Carey & Sons Ltd, lace
manufacturers, Nottingham.
Sheila Mason Collection
and John Harlow.

4 GW Price Ltd,
lace manufacturers,
Nottingham, 1938.
Sheila Mason Collection.

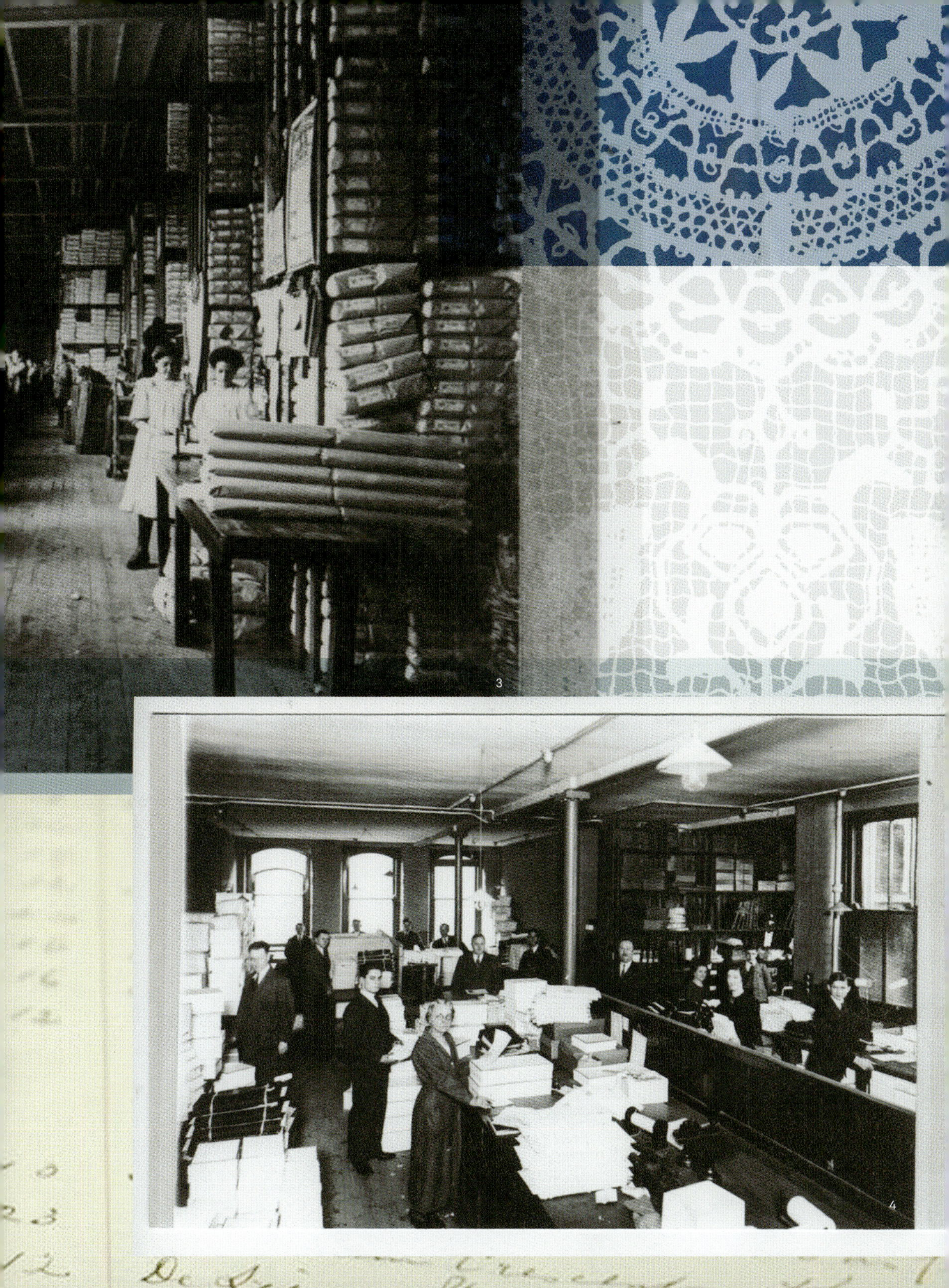

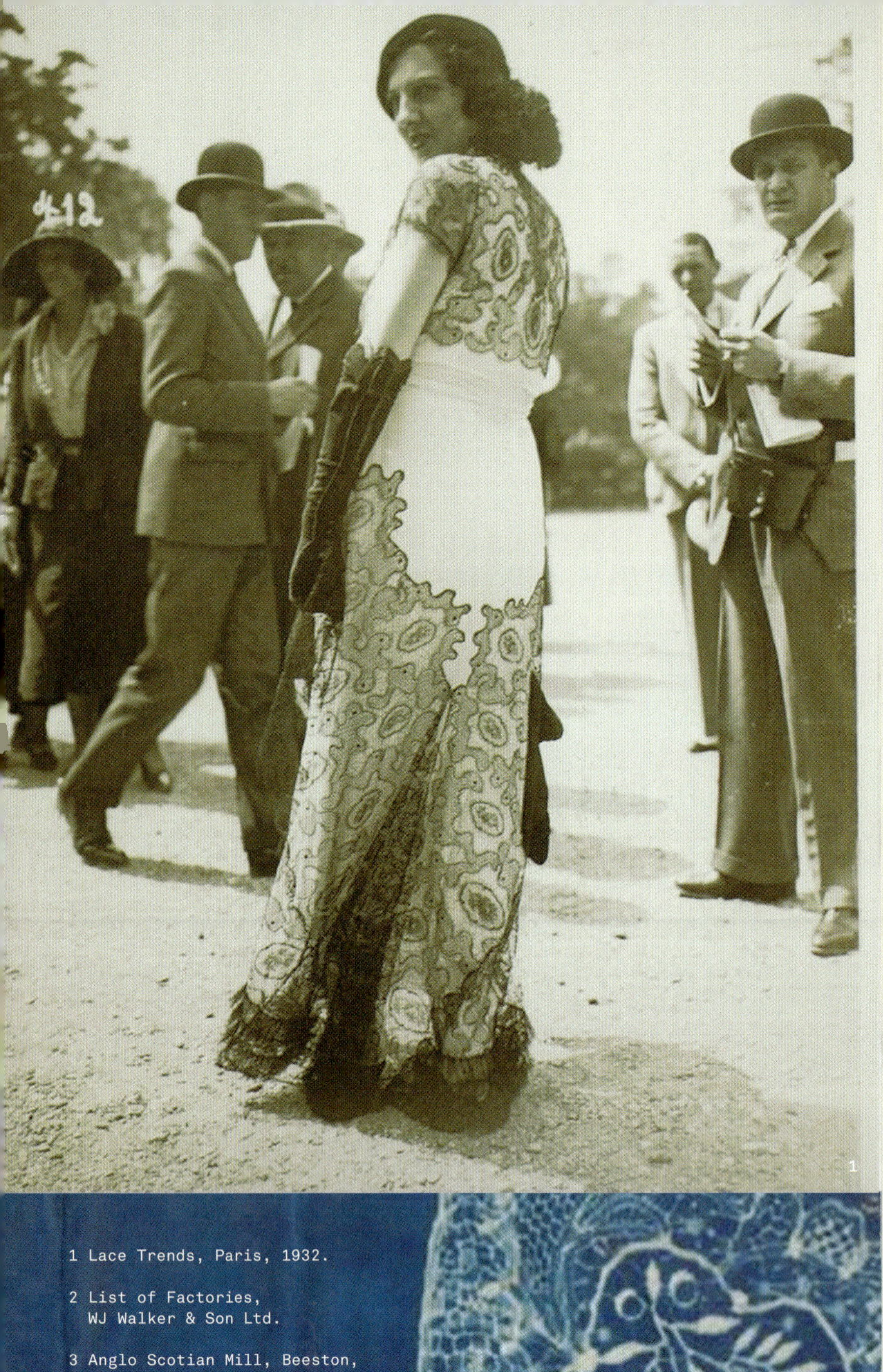

L.C.Barton. 11
Birkin & Co   B
Black Bros Ltd
Arthur Beesley
Bentley & Clif
W.B.Baggaley .
Cuckson Haselo
J.Fearfield Lt
Fisk & Co (Ba
Ernest Fewkes
A.C.Gill Ltd.
John E Hand .
Harry Johnson
George Noble.
Henry Priestle
Arthur Phelps.
G.W.Price.
E.&.A.Rishards
Simon May & Co
E.B.Sander & C
A.Tardif   60
Frank Tatham
Tathan & Co.
G. Adcock
Levin Bros

1 Lace Trends, Paris, 1932.

2 List of Factories,
  WJ Walker & Son Ltd.

3 Anglo Scotian Mill, Beeston,
  Nottingham, designed by James
  Huckerby, built for Francis
  Wilkinson, 1892.

All images courtesy Nottingham
Trent University Lace Archive if
not otherwise stated, including
blueprints and samples of lace.

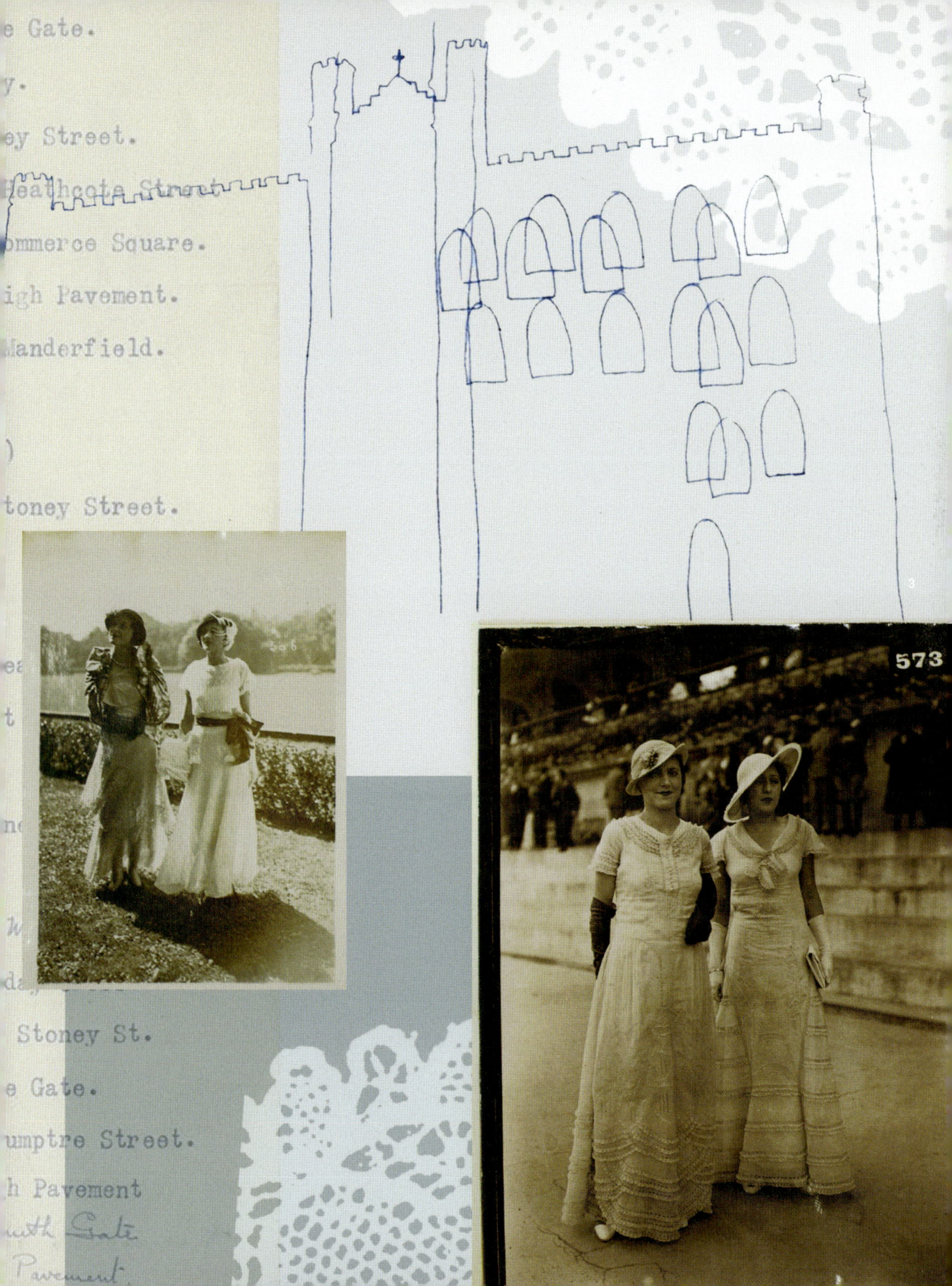
e Gate.
y.
ey Street.
Heathcote Street.
ommerce Square.
igh Pavement.
Manderfield.
)
toney Street.
ea
t
ne
W,
da
Stoney St.
e Gate.
umptre Street.
h Pavement
uth Gate
Pavement.
573

HERE

Nottingham City Museums and Galleries

Judith Edgar

In July 1878 Nottingham's first publicly owned Museum and Art Gallery opened at Nottingham Castle with the expressed intention of providing a prestigious showcase for Nottingham machine lace, alongside fine examples of art and craft from the past and present, to inspire designers in the then thriving lace industry. The Castle that stands today is in fact a seventeenth century Ducal Palace built on the site of the former Medieval Castle. The Palace was gutted by fire in the 1831 reform act riots and was remodelled in the 1870s to become the Museum that we see today.

The impetus for the Museum came from the South Kensington Museum—later the Victoria and Albert Museum (V&A)—and followed the earlier success of a temporary loan exhibition in the Exchange Buildings in the centre of Nottingham. This ran from 1872–1877 and from the outset, lace was seen to be an important element; Sir Henry Cole, a key Victorian visionary stated at the time:

> Such an exhibition ought to represent thoroughly the principal industry of the town so that Nottingham should be a centre where the history of the Lace trade could be read by the best examples and this should be for all time and not merely a transient undertaking....[1]

Amongst the exhibition loans was a large collection of hand-made lace from South Kensington Museum and a collection put together by the Nottingham Chamber of Commerce. Both were later acquired by the newly-opened Castle Museum and they formed the core of a permanent collection.

Many Castle Museum Committee members were prominent figures in the lace trade as well as being Town Councillors (Oldknow, Birkin, Vickers, Cropper, Felkin and others) and naturally they were eager to build a permanent lace collection for the city. A resolution passed by the committee in 1879 stated:

Two samples of the earliest known machine-made lace, the outline is embroidered by hand, c. 1769, made by Robert Frost of Nottingham. Courtesy Nottingham City Museums and Galleries (NCM 1878-252/1,4).

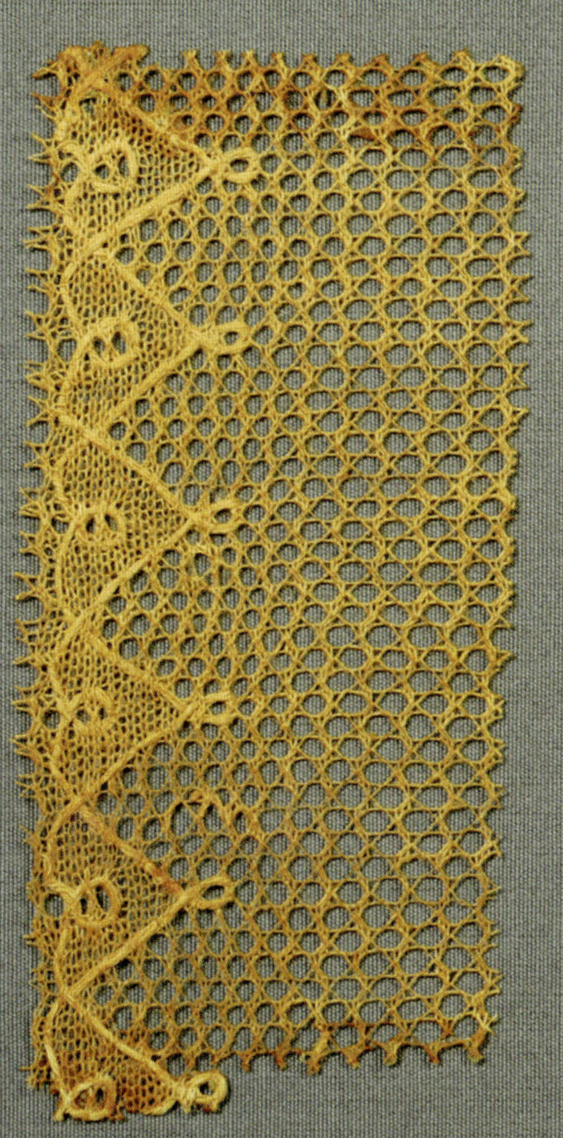
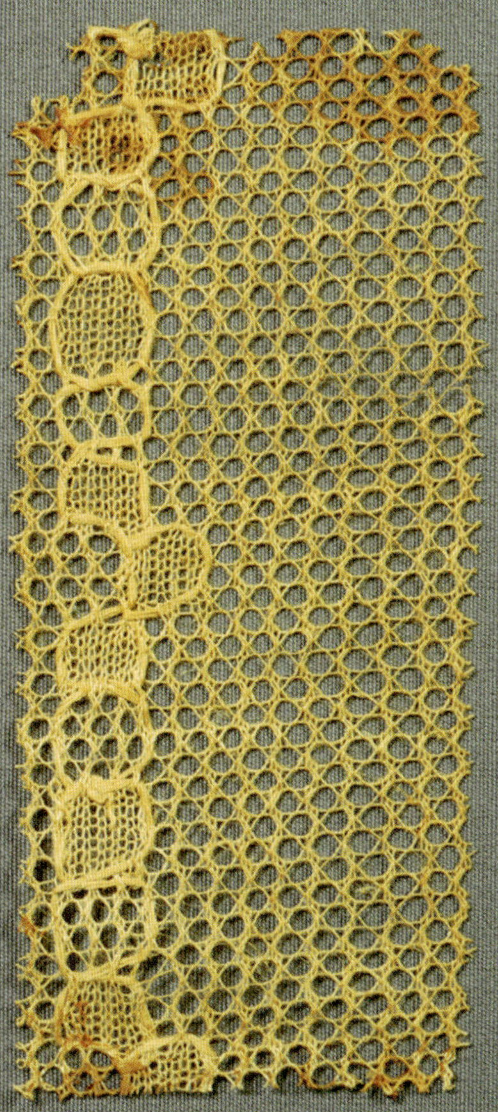

That means be taken to establish a permanent collection of Ancient and Modern Laces, and that application be made to those persons likely to assist in the same.... It is very important that Nottingham should be possessed of a good representative collection of hand-made Lace, and the Committee are desirous of making this department of the Museum as complete as possible....[2]

The earliest lace acquisitions were actually made three years before the Castle Museum opened in 1878. The 'Emperor of All the Russias' presented to the town "a fine collection of real lace, made in the north of Russia".[3] These 150 items were accessioned in 1883 and along with the 1888 purchase of Russian white work constitute "the most impressive collection of Russian peasant lace and embroidery (particularly drawn-threadwork) in Britain".[4]

The 637 pieces of machine-made lace assembled by the Nottingham Chamber of Commerce for display at the Exchange Buildings (mentioned above) were accessioned in 1878. These include examples of all the various types of early machine-made lace but perhaps the items of greatest importance are the ten patterned pieces of lace by Robert Frost of Nottingham, four of which (dating from 1769) are the earliest known examples of machine-made lace. Also included in the collection are Warp lace dating from 1785 to 1851, pieces of Bobbinet invented by John Heathcoat in around 1809 and the 520 examples of Leavers lace from 1837. These fine examples comprehensively represent the early development of the type most closely associated with Nottingham.

There are more than 100 lace sample books in the collection, dating from circa 1830 to 1985, containing over 50,000 individual pieces of lace. The first positively dated book is from 1841, by the firm Hill & Swanwick and contains 368 samples of white cotton warp-frame lace. Another sample book, produced by Mallet and Birkin, was found buried under the foundation stone of the Nottingham Corporation Water Board Offices and is dated prior to 1847. This sample book contains the piece of lace which was used to inspire the embossed lace pattern on the external concrete walls of Nottingham Contemporary—the 2009 award-winning gallery building.

From 1880 efforts to acquire more hand-made lace resulted in several large gifts being accepted, the first being 98 pieces from Crete and then in 1882, 144 items of hand-made lace dating from 1550 to 1860 from Italy,

Evening dress and jacket designed by H Webster and manufactured by AC Gill and Co Ltd, 'Witchcraft Lace', Warser Gate, Nottingham. 1951, ivory cotton net machine embroidered (Schiffli), ivory acetate taffeta, machine stitched, hand finished, Nottingham City Museums and Galleries (NCM 1962–43). Produced as part of the Festival Pattern Group—a unique project at the Festival of Britain involving X-ray crystallographers, designers and manufacturers, inspired by the crystal structure of the beryl.

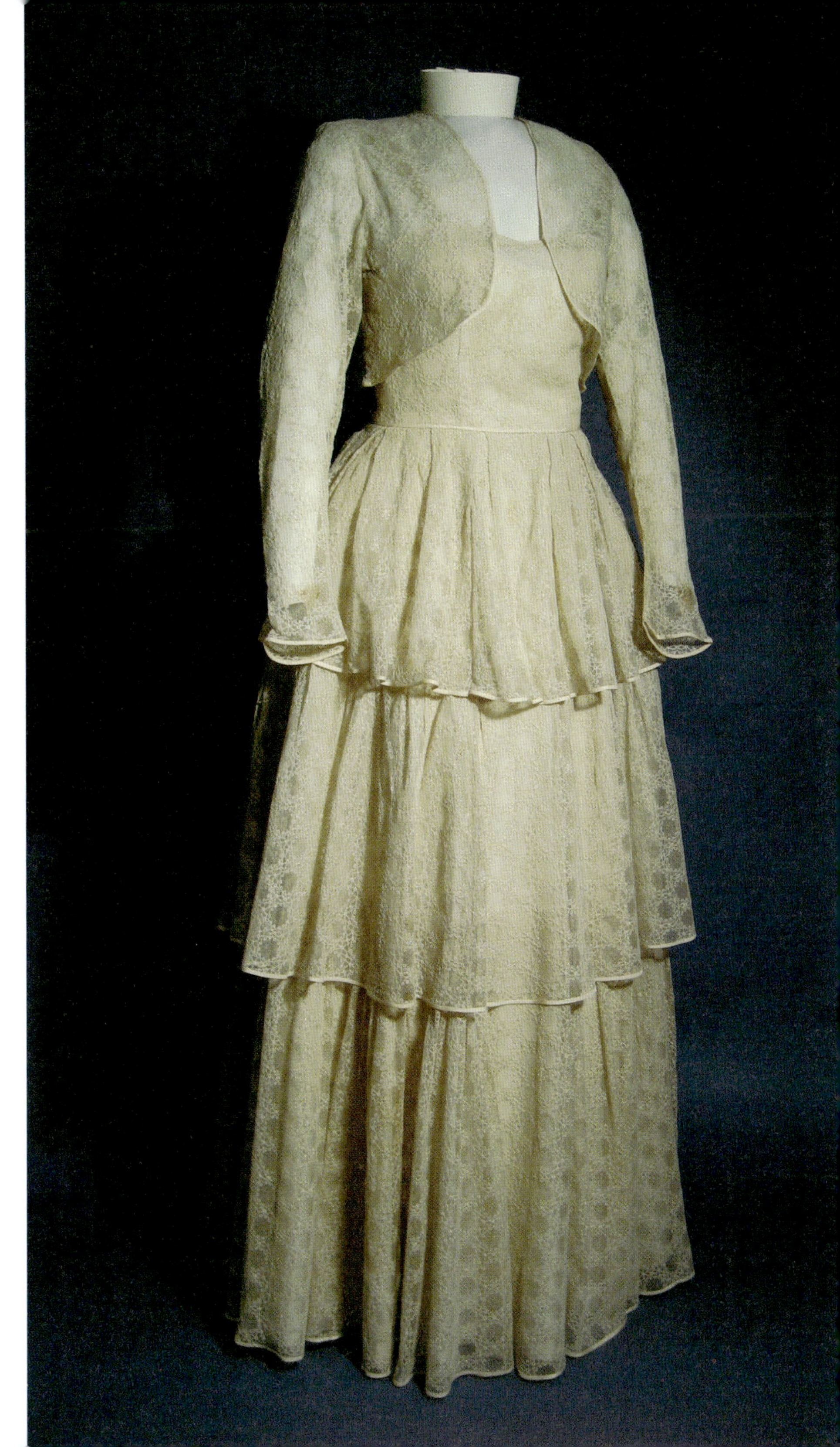

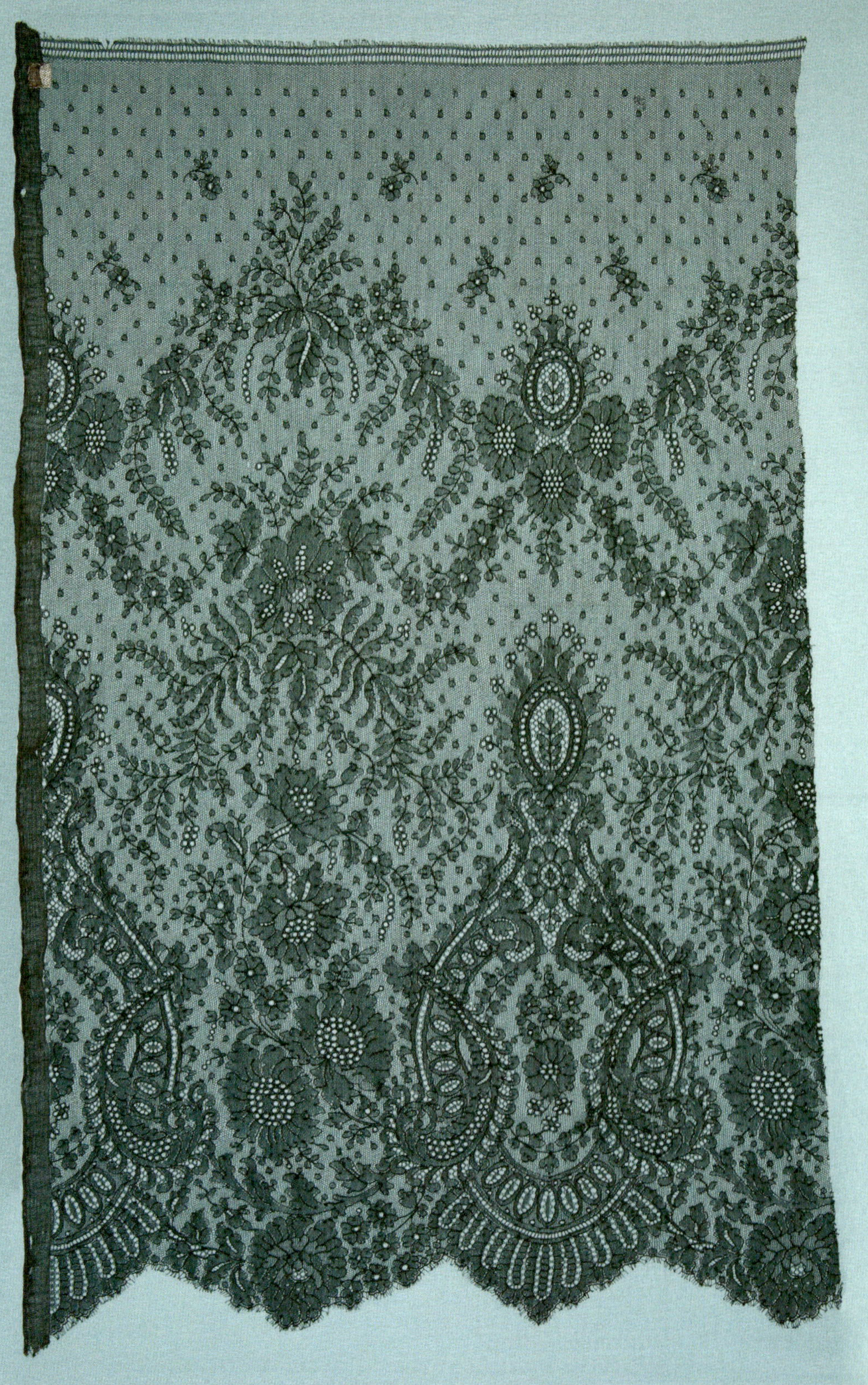

Belgium, Flanders and France. The majority of these items are borders and insertions but a Venetian collar of 1680, Lappets of Valenciennes pillow lace dated to 1730 and sleeve ruffs (one pair possibly as early as 1715) stand out as significant examples.

Many more samples of lace and lace related items have been acquired over the years, including the extensive archive from the long established firm of Birkin and over 1,000 items of costume made either wholly or principally of lace, or with important lace trimmings.

An important collection of lace machinery, acquired from prominent lace and machinery manufacturers in the late-nineteenth and early-twentieth centuries has evolved alongside the lace collection and has been displayed at the Industrial Museum, in the Stable Block at Wollaton Hall, since 1971.

Between 1976 to 2003, the lace collection itself was displayed in the Museum of Costume and Textiles on Castlegate; however, in 2012 the collection, along with the wider Costume and Textiles collection, was re-located to improved storage and research facilities at Newstead Abbey.

The strengths of the Nottingham City Museums' collection are its unique coverage of both machine-made lace and machinery, combined with the broad scope of the hand-made lace and the use of lace in numerous examples of costume and furnishings. In 2012 both the machine-made lace and the hand-made lace collections were peer reviewed by Heather Toomer and Penny Alfrey and came to the following conclusions: 'The hand-made lace collection is of national significance and of major significance both to Nottinghamshire and to the City of Nottingham'[5]; 'The machine-made lace collection is of regional, national and international significance.'[6]

The recent addition of a study suite, adjacent to the collection stores at Newstead Abbey, and initiatives such as the lace:here:now season in 2012/13, have ensured continuing high standards of care for the lace collection and begun to demonstrate its vital contribution to the telling of the internationally-important story of Nottingham's lace industry.

1. Henry Cole, Secretary of the Department of Science and Art, which administered the South Kensington Museum.
2. Castle Museum Committee Minutes, 26 November 1879.
3. Annual Report of the School of Art and Exhibition Committee, 1875–1876.
4. Pamela Smith, MA dissertation "From Goose to Firebird: the collecting, display and consumption and interpretation of Russian Peasant, kustar and art embroideries in Britain, 1880–1930", MA History of Decorative Art and Design, University of Brighton.
5. Heather Toomer, Peer Review of Nottingham Museums' Hand-made Lace Collection, 2012.
6. Penny Alfrey, Peer Review of Nottingham Museums' Machine-made Lace Collection, 2012.

Nottingham Leavers
1910–1920, silk, pattern repeat,
machine lace border, 19 cm.
Donated by Guy Birkin Ltd,
Courtesy Nottingham City Museums
and Galleries (NCM 1972–30/43)

The Nottingham Trent University Lace Archive

Amanda Briggs-Goode

The Lace Archive housed in the School of Art and Design at Nottingham Trent University (NTU) is unique in many respects; it goes beyond what might ordinarily be expected of a repository of textiles. Loose hand and machine-made lace samples sit together with products of a bygone era. The collection provides an opportunity to examine beautiful fabrics and samples of lace while unveiling insight into other interrelated issues such as education and the design process. Established at the beginnings of art school education in the UK, the Archive offers testimony of the teaching process in the Victorian era demonstrating a particular focus upon the lace design process; from technical resolve and 'draughting' to commercial product applications. Other items within the collection include a large body of design portfolios, which were acquired at European exhibitions alongside design intelligence reports to Nottingham from 'spys' in Parisian couture houses and at 'society' events; with the intention to inspire new designs, as well as offer an advantage through commercial acumen.

The social history of the lace industry is also evident through business records and documentation where, for example, you might note how gender roles were defined through the various jobs within the industry and how economic value was assigned to each discreet function within the making and manufacture of lace, as well as the business operating costs. The substantial library of books also documents the industrial heritage of manufactured lace developed in Nottingham and surrounding counties. The Archive demonstrates the rich and valuable heritage of Nottingham Lace and the city's unique and central position in the development of this now global industry.

In the mid-nineteenth century hand-made lace was an expensive commodity and considered a luxury item. The mechanisation of lace production meant that it could be democratised, enabling the Victorian middle classes to consume what was previously unaffordable. Lace

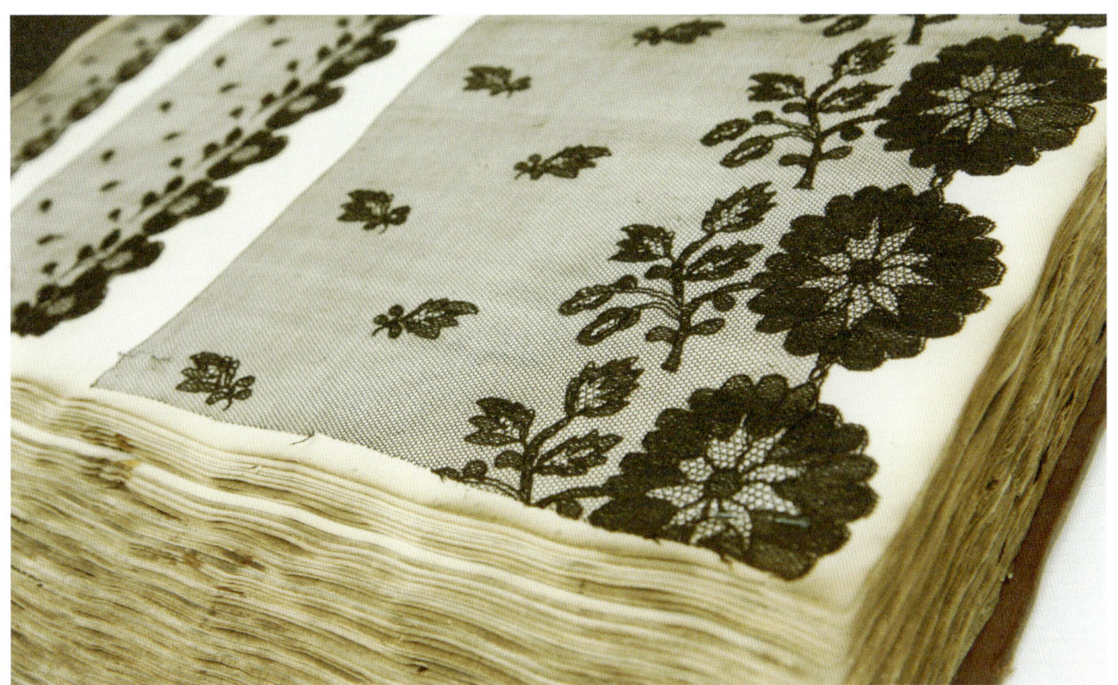

was of practical, economic and social significance, and the relationship between what was often described, as ˝real versus imitation˝ lace was hotly debated in consumer and women's magazines of the time.[1] To ensure that Nottingham lace convinced the consumer, an investment in design and designers was necessary. The Archive of today is the result of benefactions from the past industry's support and belief in the need for a School of Art and Design.

> To us, as a peculiarly manufacturing nation the connection between art and manufacture is most important, and for this merely economic reason (were there no higher motive) it equally imports us to encourage design since it tends to advance the humblest pursuits of industry.[2]

This quote is taken from a Report of a Select Committee on Arts and Manufactures in 1836, established to address the concern over the loss of overseas markets despite the technical excellence of British products.

The select committee concluded that investment in British design education was the missing ingredient which would help to quell the

Machine and hand lace sample book, containing mid-nineteenth century lace samples. Donated by William Felkin.

rising tide of foreign competition. As a result, the Government Schools of Design were created, the first of which was the Royal College of Art in 1837, followed by Manchester and York in 1842 and in 1843 the Nottingham Government School of Design was founded. These Schools were granted aid on the conditions that they followed the 'metropolitan' curriculum and that they could raise funds from the local industry and benefactors. In Nottingham a committee had been established with 52 members including lace manufacturers Richard Birkin and Thomas Adams amongst others. The first school was opened at the People's Hall in Beck Lane with the mission to "provide elementary instruction in design for manufactures, and in the history, principles and practice of ornamental art".[3] Nottingham was ahead of this interest in design education as drawing classes had been established since the opening of The Mechanics Institute in 1837.[4] The School of Design occupied several sites around the city until the foundation stone was laid on Waverley Street for a purpose built design school in 1843, the building opened in 1865. This building called Waverley Building still forms one of the main sites for the School of Art and Design today. The impact of the teaching and training of design and technical skills for the lace industry in the school of art and design is contentious, while there is evidence of the success of design in the many awards that were given to the school and many of its design students there are also clear challenges to this through various institutional documents and publications which questioned the quality of the education the lace designers were receiving.[5] What is clear is that the School of Design has continued to develop, grow and succeed to be recognised as the School of Art and Design as part of NTU.

The minutes of the early school of design identified the need for both textile examples and a library of text books to support instruction. As many of the governors were lace manufacturers, support for developing a teaching collection was forthcoming.[6] William Felkin, the author of *History of the Machine-Wrought Hosiery and Lace Manufactures*, "presented the school with four pattern books containing thousands of cotton and silk point laces".[7] Later, significant donations were made by the British Lace Federation of designs and drafts by the renowned lace designer William Pegg (1864–1946) and this was followed by donations from lace manufactures; Thomas Adams, Zachariah Sketchley and, by the son of GW Price, of the Price Memorial Collection.[8]

Records of donations to the Archive were either not made or have been lost or destroyed over the intervening years and therefore knowing

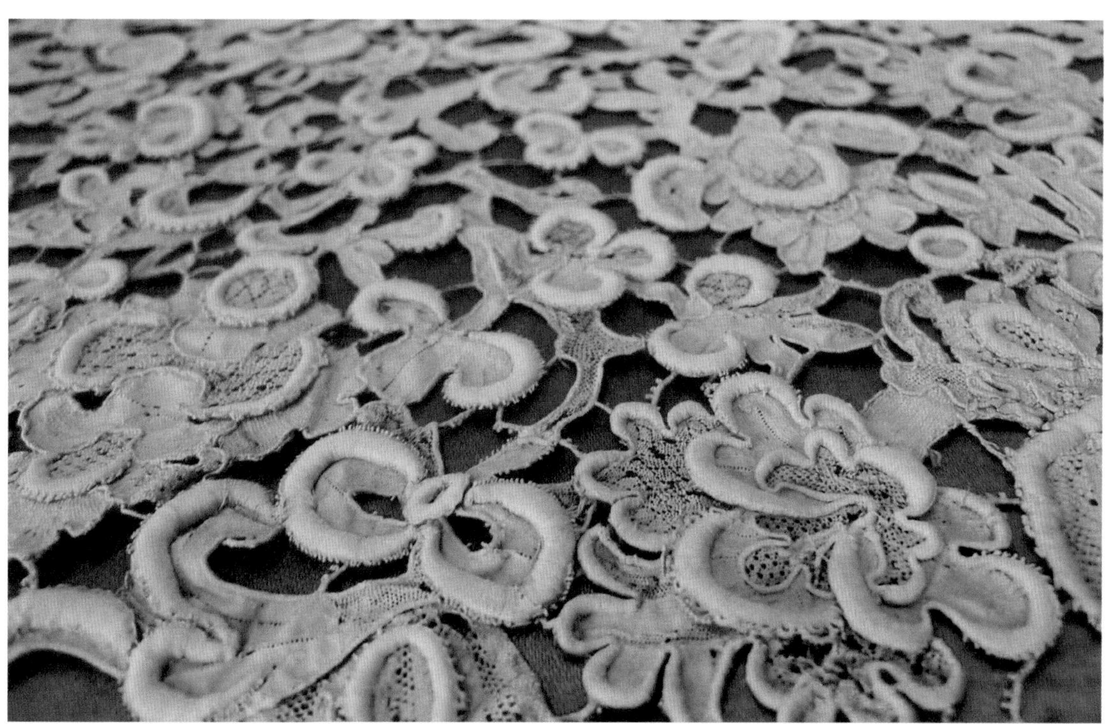

in what order things arrived into the Archive is sadly not possible. However, the Archive as we know it today, has a vast variety of resources including samples of hand-made and machine-made lace mainly from the UK and Europe; design portfolios; sample books; text books; business records, photographs, some machine parts and a small amount of film footage, examples of lace 'prickings' and jacquard cards. There are around 75,000 items in the Archive and therefore a snapshot of some of these will be described here.

There are many samples of hand-made lace in the collection and students were required to imitate them as closely as possible. The most significant piece of hand-made lace in the Archive is a late-seventeenth century panel from a *chasuble*, which is a priest's ceremonial outer garment. The *chasuble* was created using a technique known as 'gros-point' and is likely to have been produced in Venice. In this form of lacemaking small stitches are used to create the flat base cloth and then wadding is added to produce an embossed, three-dimensional effect. The wadding is then covered in stitches and further decorated

Seventeenth century Venetian gros point *chasuble* with double eagle crest and floral design.

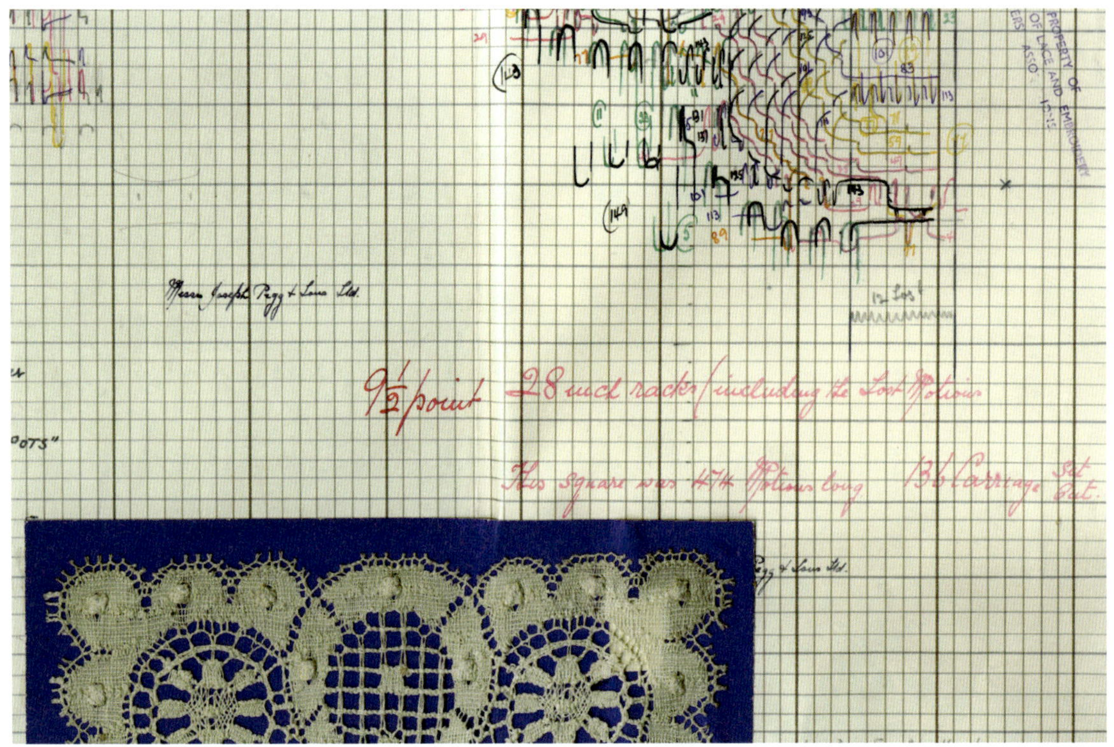

1

with picots to embellish and disguise the padding. This type of lace would have required highly skilled embroiders and have taken vast amounts of time to make. Gros-point lace was often described as looking like carved ivory due to the considerable skills of those capable of stitching out such smooth and even forms. Due to the high cost of such items they were often repaired several times and as such become a montage of several different makers, stitch and thread types, and this becomes more or less obvious depending upon the skill of the Lacemaker.

The Design Process

In the Archive we have many examples of draughts, which offer us a view of the design process for creating lace from idea to manufacture. This process was a team effort relying upon both the designer and the draughtsman. Such draughts are complex and mathematical and required an eight year apprenticeship to become fully qualified. The designer's role was to develop new and creative design ideas with awareness of

1 Twentieth century technical
  drawings of lace, 1943.
  GW Price Ltd Memorial Collection.

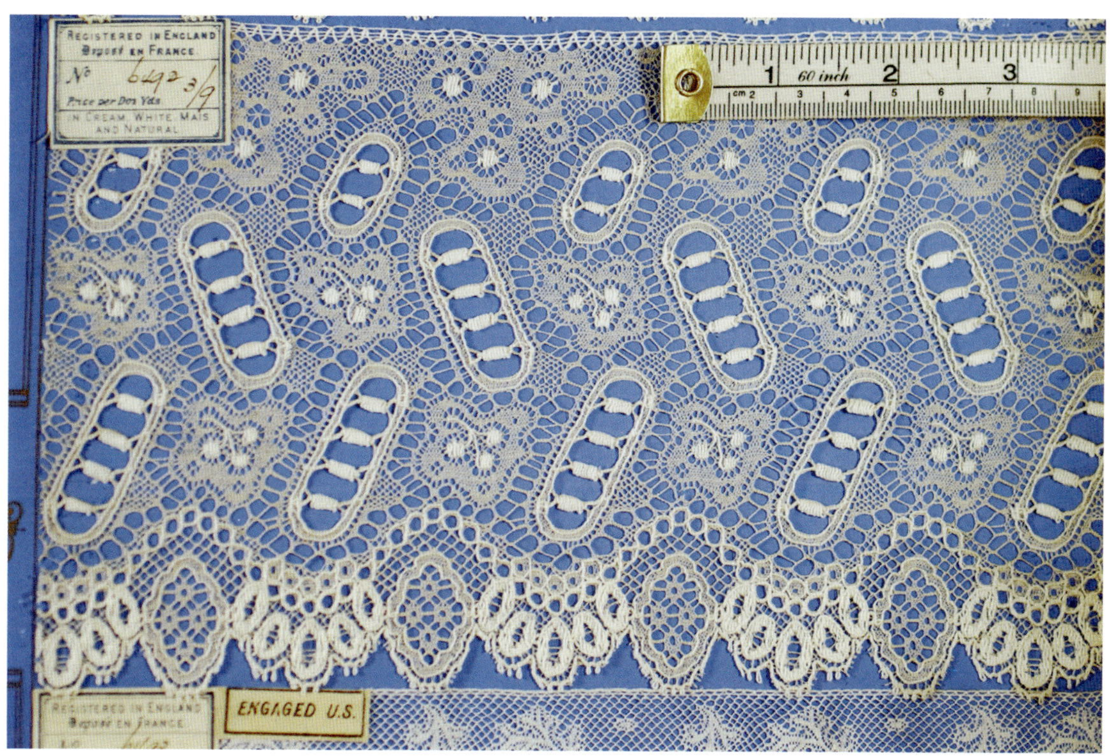

2

production processes and technologies. While the draftsman took responsibility for taking the design and interpreting it ready for production, the draftsman's role was to translate the design onto a highly complex chart. This informed how the jacquard cards were punched, which in turn controlled the movement of each bar and ultimately guided each thread. The draft was produced on a type of graph paper, several times larger than the design. The design was then drawn onto the draft with the draughtsman recording every movement of the beam and warp thread. After this has been completed, the design was 'read off' which means that the numbers are placed onto a grid to indicate the position of each thread in the pattern. Every movement of the thread was shown on the draft and is indicated numerically upon the figure sheet .

The students had been taught using a government led curriculum and the previous design 'bible' the *Grammar of Ornament* began to be superseded by new approaches influenced by the emerging

2 Late-nineteenth century
  lace sample.

Overleaf
Early-twentieth century
design portfolio.
GW Price Ltd Memorial Collection,
Patent No 782821, May 1933.

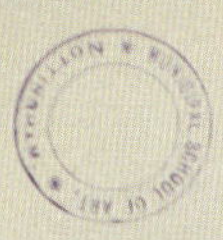

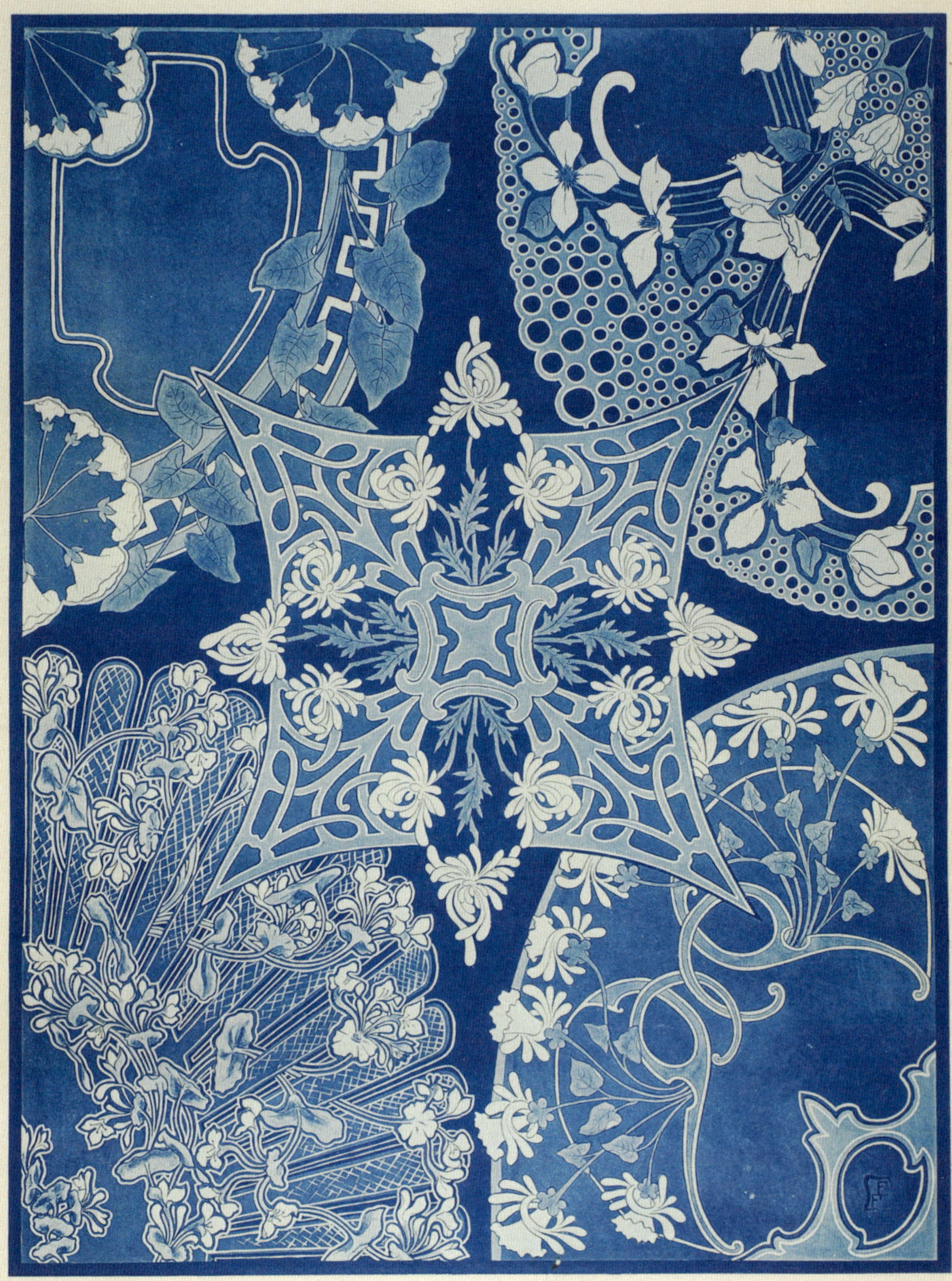

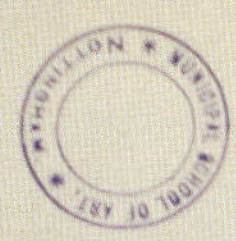

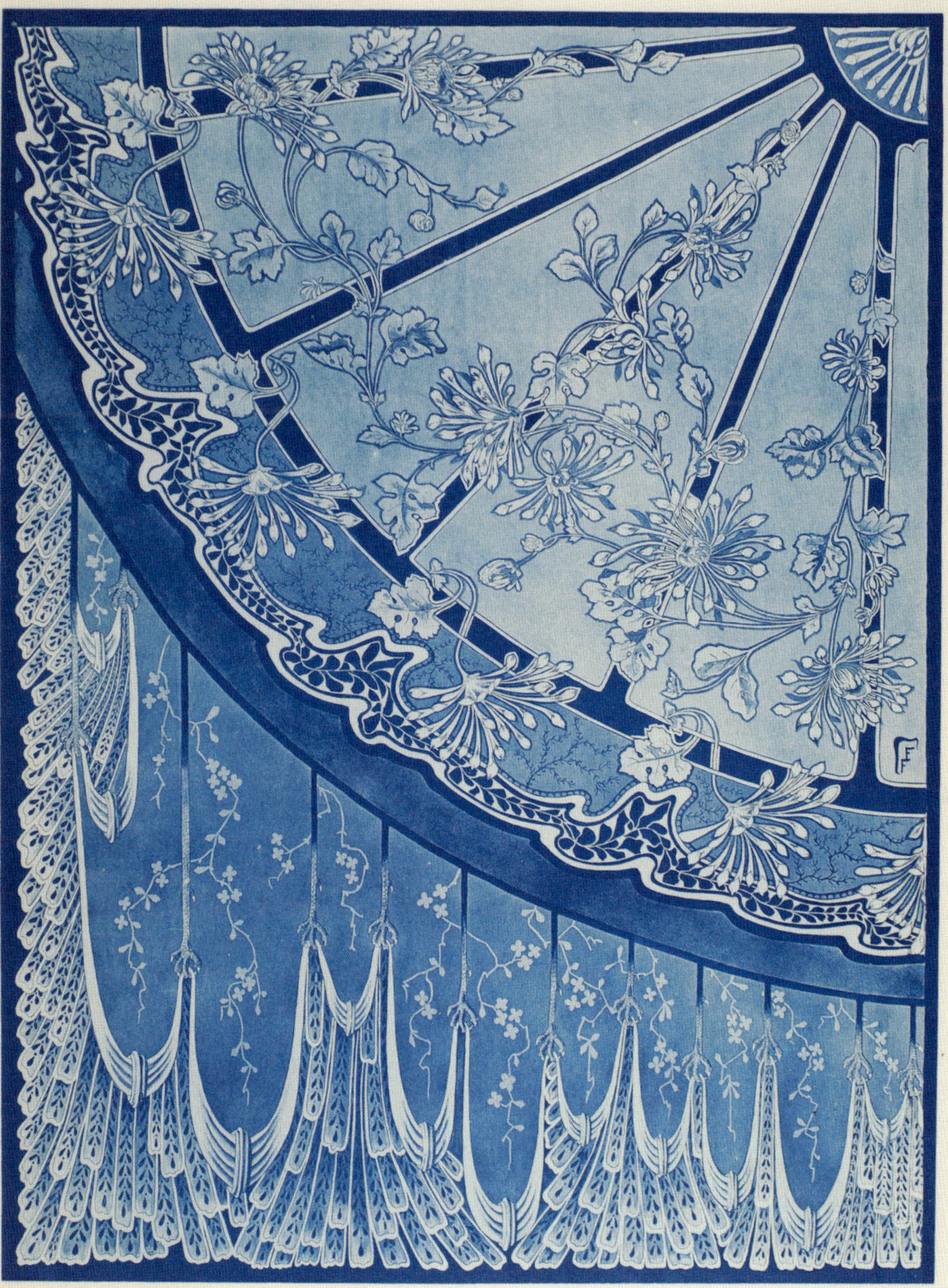

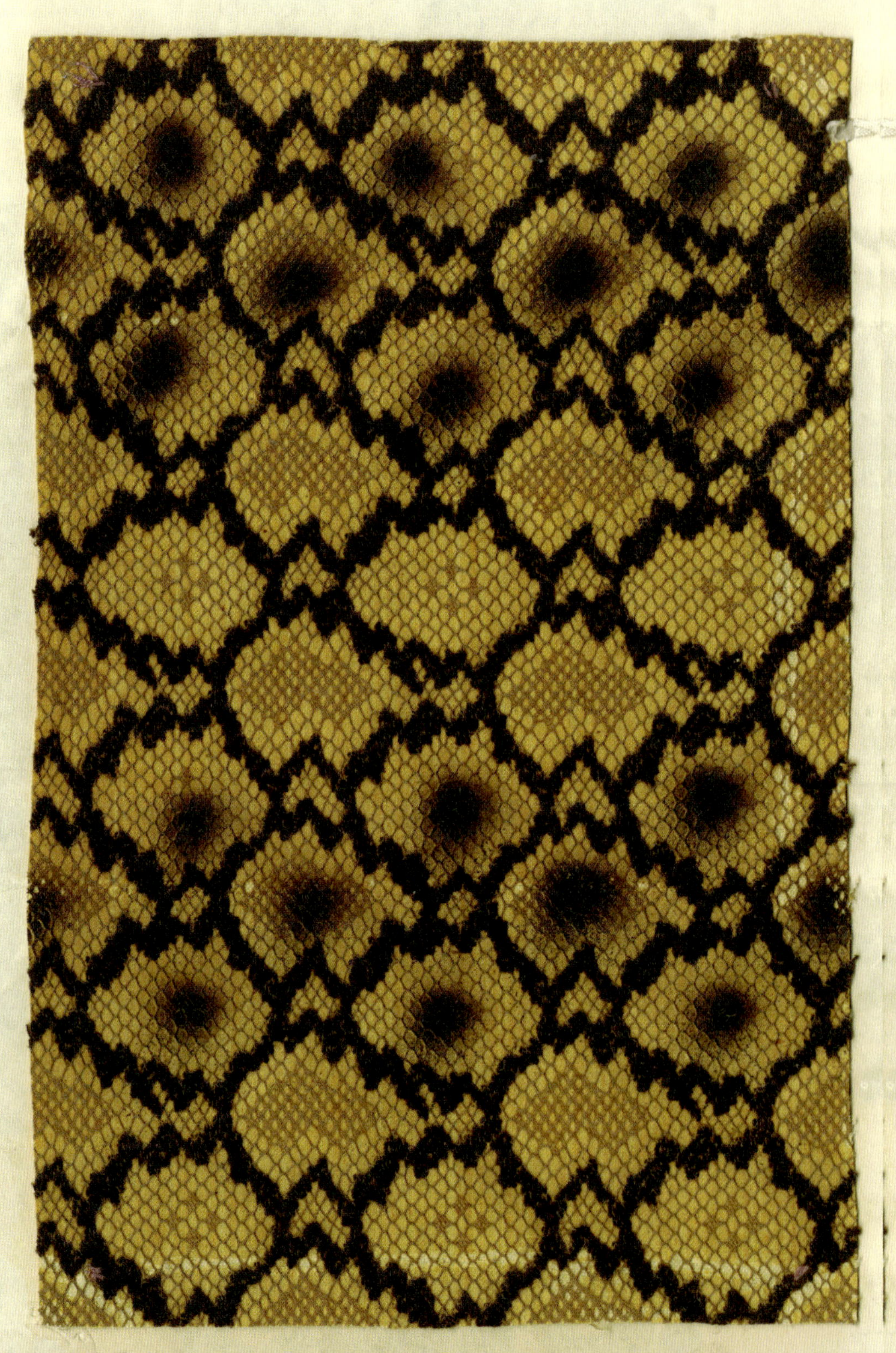

PATENTS AND DESIGNS ACTS, 1907 to 1932.

...ate of Registration of Design.

THE PATENT OFFICE: DESIGNS BRANCH,
25, SOUTHAMPTON BUILDINGS,
CHANCERY LANE, LONDON, W.C.2.

Number of Registration 782821.

This is to certify that the Design, of which a copy is annexed, has been registered in Class twelve as of the 2nd day of May, 1933, in respect of the application of such Design to a sheet of textile material for use as a substitute for fancy leather

in pursuance of and subject to the provisions of the Patents and Designs Acts, 1907 to 1932, and the Designs Rules, 1932.

M. F. LINDLEY,
*Comptroller-General of Patents,
Designs and Trade Marks.*

W. Mycroft.

~~Copy~~
~~date,~~
~~furth~~

RULE 64.—(1)

(2)

(R1469) Wt 1884

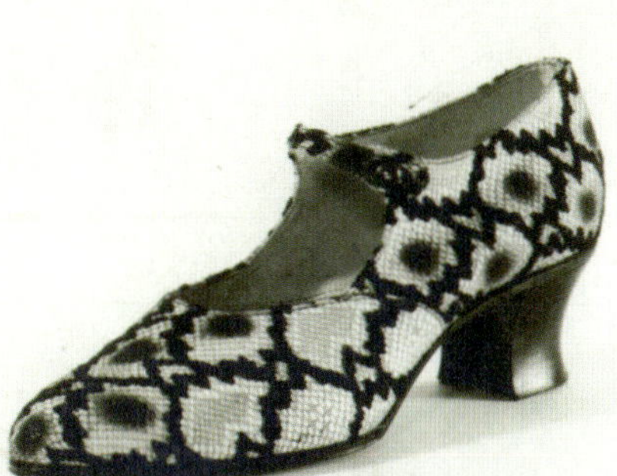

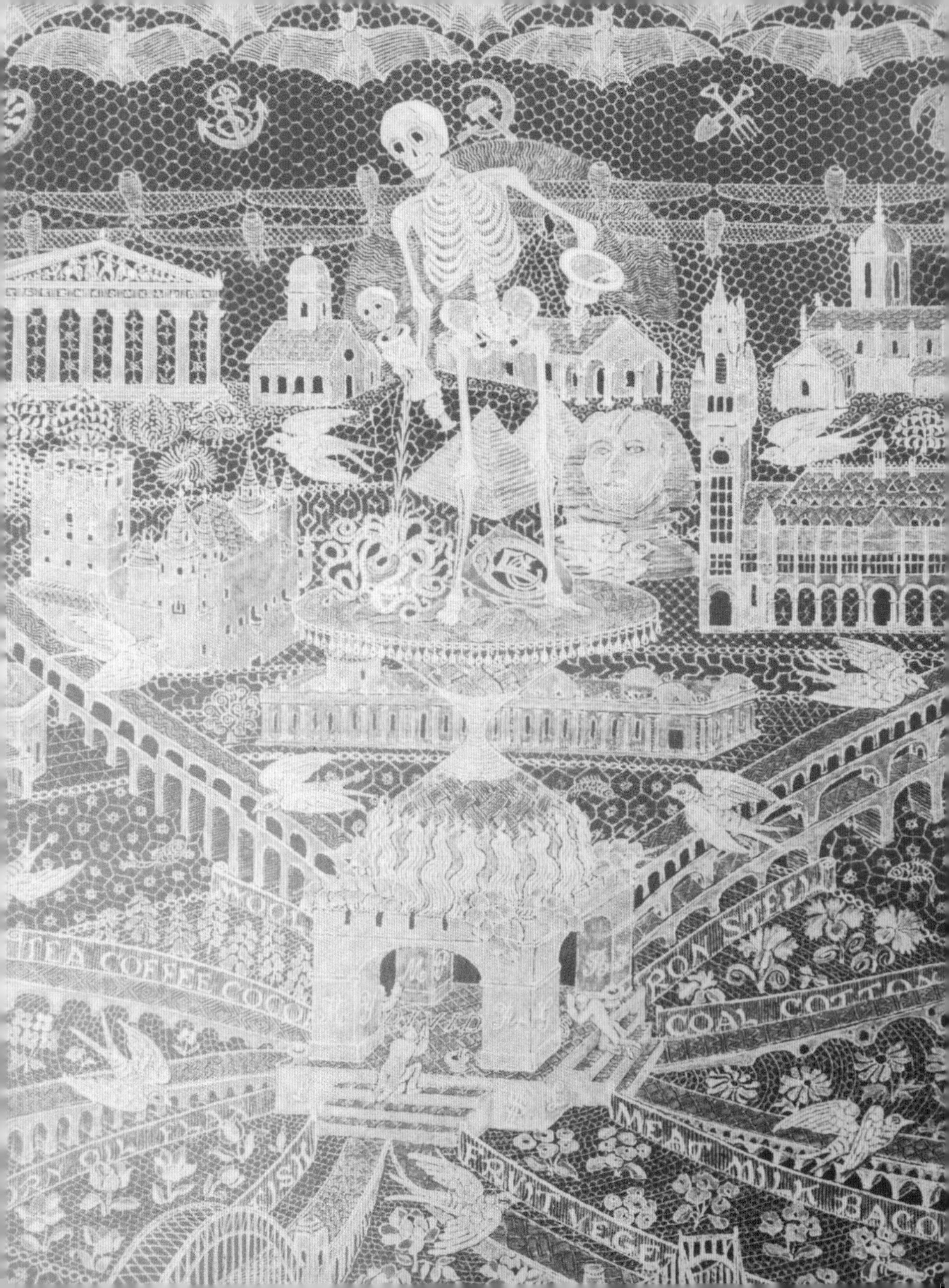

TEA
COFFEE
COCOA
WOOL
IRON
STEEL
COAL
COTTON

fashion system and an increase in communication methods of new styles in the form of magazines.[9] In studios the purchase of design portfolios with drawings and photographs of diverse subjects from sea-life to architecture and of course florals enabled a new perspective on visual information and this empowered designers to begin to develop more creative design responses, leading to what became known as "novelty laces". Other intriguing and novel designs within the collection are the attempts to create a lace which when applied to a spray painted man-made leather material imitates snake skin. In the Archive, these designs are presented as patents (782821) with accompanying product application photograph. Earnshaw discusses these samples as having "an air of desperation about them".[10] She comments that these were submitted in the early 1930s as a time when economic depression was hitting European and American markets and when the huge loss of men due to the First World War was impacting upon workforces. Despite these factors, I find these pieces are a testimony to creative and diverse thinking of the designers and product developers working in Nottingham during this period.

A significant collection within the Archive is The Pegg Collection which was donated post Second World War by the British Lace Federation. William Pegg (1864–1946) was an award winning student in the School of Art and Design (1883); he was also later applauded as a commercial designer. His strong political beliefs led him to design lace which sits within the Russian Constructivist textile tradition, essentially designing lace with a communist agenda. In the Archive we hold several designs from this collection—*hammer and sickle* and *kremlin*—the details evident in all of these pieces demonstrate Pegg's considerable skills not only in designing lace but also his ability to create flowing seamless patterns, through his understanding of scale, proportion and movement. All these demark him as a leader in his field at this time. The complexity and the conceptual nature of the design for a lace panel: *Needlepoint Lace and Embroidery Panel recording the Abortive Economic Conference of 64 Nations in London 1933, with its Concomitant Orgy of Destruction* demonstrate his ability to synthesise ideology (political and religious), technology, and the order and organisation of visual information to create a novel and dramatic statement. Not to mention the level of research involved (in pre-Internet days) to assist in the creation of geographic and architectural icons which include: eight bridges, 64 buildings or monuments, and 64 flags to represent each of the countries who attended the conference.

William Pegg, design for needlepoint lace and embroidery panel recording the abortive economic conference of 64 nations in London, 1933.

While lace design is no longer taught at NTU as a specific design discipline, the Lace Archive with its rich textile heritage continues to inspire creative practice for students and staff across the School of Art and Design, as well as visitors. The Archive is inspirational and has been used to stimulate art and design projects including lace:here:now and other exhibitions. Researchers and practitioners have also used the Archive. In particular the work of Joy Buttress, who gained her PhD in 2013, and whose research into "The Metaphorical Value of Lace in Contemporary Art: The Transformative Process of a Practice-Led Inquiry" has led to insights into how historically informed creative practice can transform our understanding of the value of archives and in the process, enrich our interpretation. A current PhD study by Nicola Donovan, whose research is entitled "Out of the Archive—On the Development of a Dialogical Art Practice", initiated by Nottingham's Lace Heritage seeks to challenge how lace is interpreted and exhibited in museum contexts. Artist Danica Maier was commissioned to produce an artwork by the German women's organisation GEDOK in Karlsruhe, Germany in 2009. GEDOK specifically selected Maier as an artist who works with lace to create an artwork that celebrated a 40 year town partnership with Nottingham. Maier produced *Midlands and Tooraloorals*, 2009, an installation that took inspiration from motifs found in the NTU Lace Archive. It is our intention that we will continue to use this remarkable Archive to inspire designers and artists of the future, as it was historically intended.

1. Brompton, R, "Lilies and Lace: An investigation into the relationship between hand and machine-made costume lace through fashionable middle class consumption 1851–1887", PhD unpublished thesis, Nottingham Trent University, 2002.
2. Lyon, R, *A History of Nottingham College of Art and Design*, Nottingham: George Searson Ltd, 1970.
3. Jones, C, *The History of Nottingham School of Design*, Nottingham: Nottingham Trent University, 1993 p 14.
4. Jones, C, *The History of Nottingham School of Design*, 1993.
5. Debates about the effectiveness of the education are evident through a range of documents from the School of Art and Design, records of the borough of Nottingham and the records of Nottingham Chamber of Commerce. This is clearly articulated in S Mason, *Nottingham Lace 1760s–1950s*, Nottingham: Sheila Mason, second edition, 2010, pp. 181–189.
6. Smith, B, "Nottingham Trent University's Lace Archive", *Textiles Magazine*, Issue 1.
7. Felkin first published this book in 1867; private correspondence with Sheila Mason, May 2013.
8. Correspondence with Sheila Mason, May 2013.
9. Owen Jones formulated the decorative arts principles which became the teaching frameworks for the Government School of Design and it is based upon these propositions that he published *The Grammar of Ornament* in 1856.
10. Earnshaw, P, "Lace for your Shoes: Impractical Vanity", *The Bulletin of the Needle and Bobbin Club*, vol. 70, 1987.

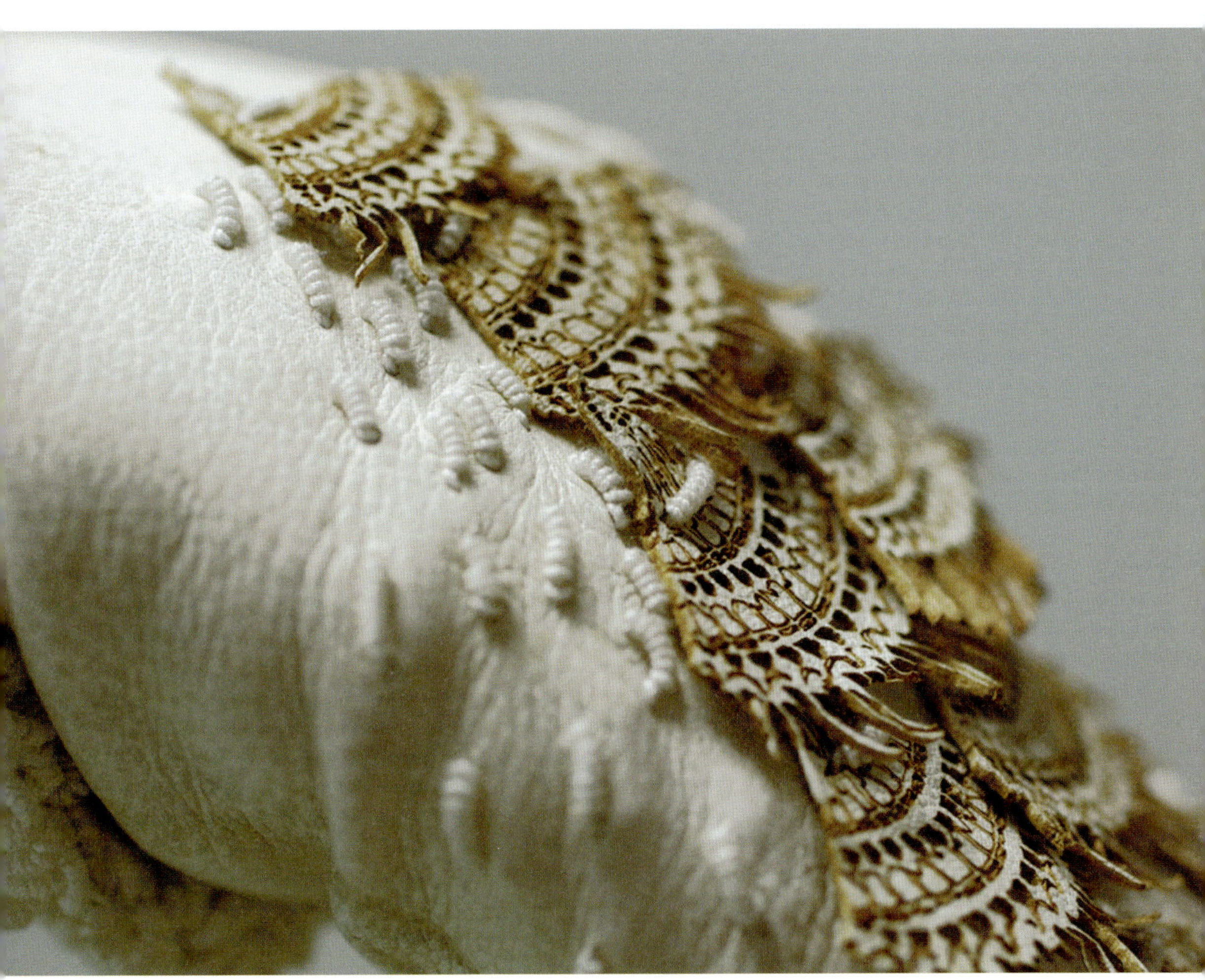

Joy Buttress
<u>Glove One</u>
2012, vintage leather
glove, silk thread, hand
embroidery, laser etched.

NOW

Journeys in Lace—
Parts One and Two
Amanda Briggs-Goode

"Journeys in Lace—Parts One and Two" was conceived as part of the lace:here:now season, which evolved from a series of discussions between Nottingham Trent University's (NTU) School of Art and Design and Nottingham Castle Museum and Art Gallery. lace:here:now incorporated a number of events organised in recognition of lace heritage and the value with which our Archive is viewed. These events took place at key venues across the city during the autumn and winter of 2012–2013. This offered us an opportunity to showcase the NTU Lace Archive and increase its usage by current students and staff, in order to give them inspiration for developing future design and artwork and to raise their awareness of lacemaking culture and technology. The work which has been produced as a result has formed the basis of "Journeys in Lace—Parts One and Two".

Journeys in Lace—Part One was exhibited at the Wallner Gallery, Lakeside Arts Centre, Nottingham. This exhibition allowed both academic and technical staff to access some of the rich and diverse artefacts held within the Archive, to explore their essence through a range of creative practices, and to reinterpret these historic objects from a new audience point of view. Visiting the Archive is a unique and sensorial experience. Its aesthetic beauty and the unusual olfaction are mediated by the grandiose scale of the collection and its emblematic value as a bygone era and the sheer scale of the production. All this, however, is only the tip of an iceberg of lace manufacturing in Nottingham. Visitors to the Archive find the vast quantity of lace held within it overwhelming. Thus when we invited staff to the Archive to choose their inspirational pieces, we did an initial sift—wanting to show the diversity of what the Archive has to offer to give them a starting point to establish their interest. While the participants considered the pieces, using mobile phones and digital cameras to capture their personal delights, we talked through the histories, the processes and the value of the

Opposite
Katherine Townsend
Plastron—Light 1 & 2
Silk viscose, inkjet and
dévorè print, 90 x 60 cm.

Overleaf left
Debbie Gonet
Three Fragments
Silk smooth chiffon, tulle, knitted
fabric, cotton, silk, rayon thread,
hand and machine-embroidery.

Overleaf right
Amanda Briggs-Goode
Circles of Lace
Silk, chiffon, acid dyes,
digital print, 70 x 70 cm.

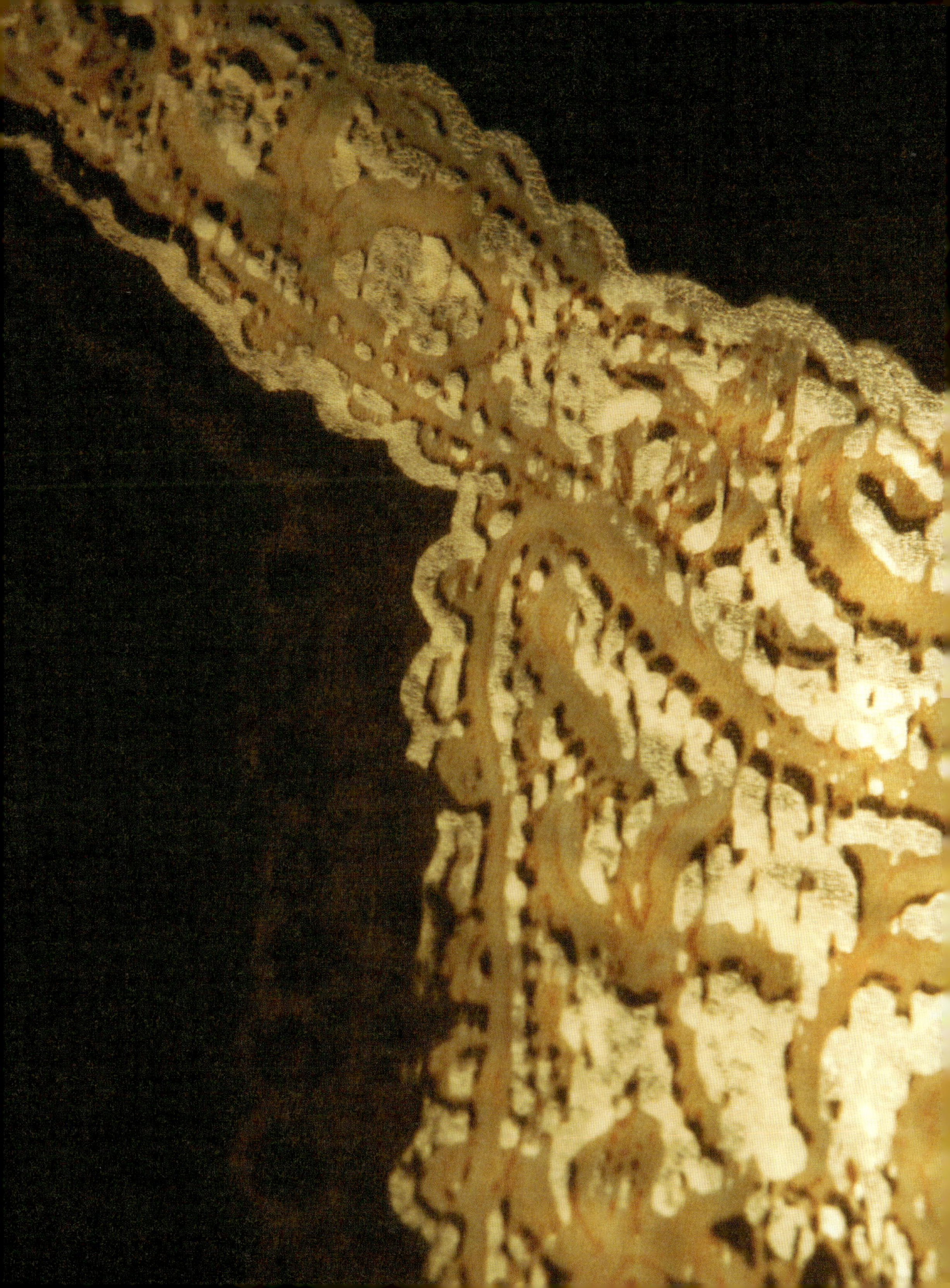

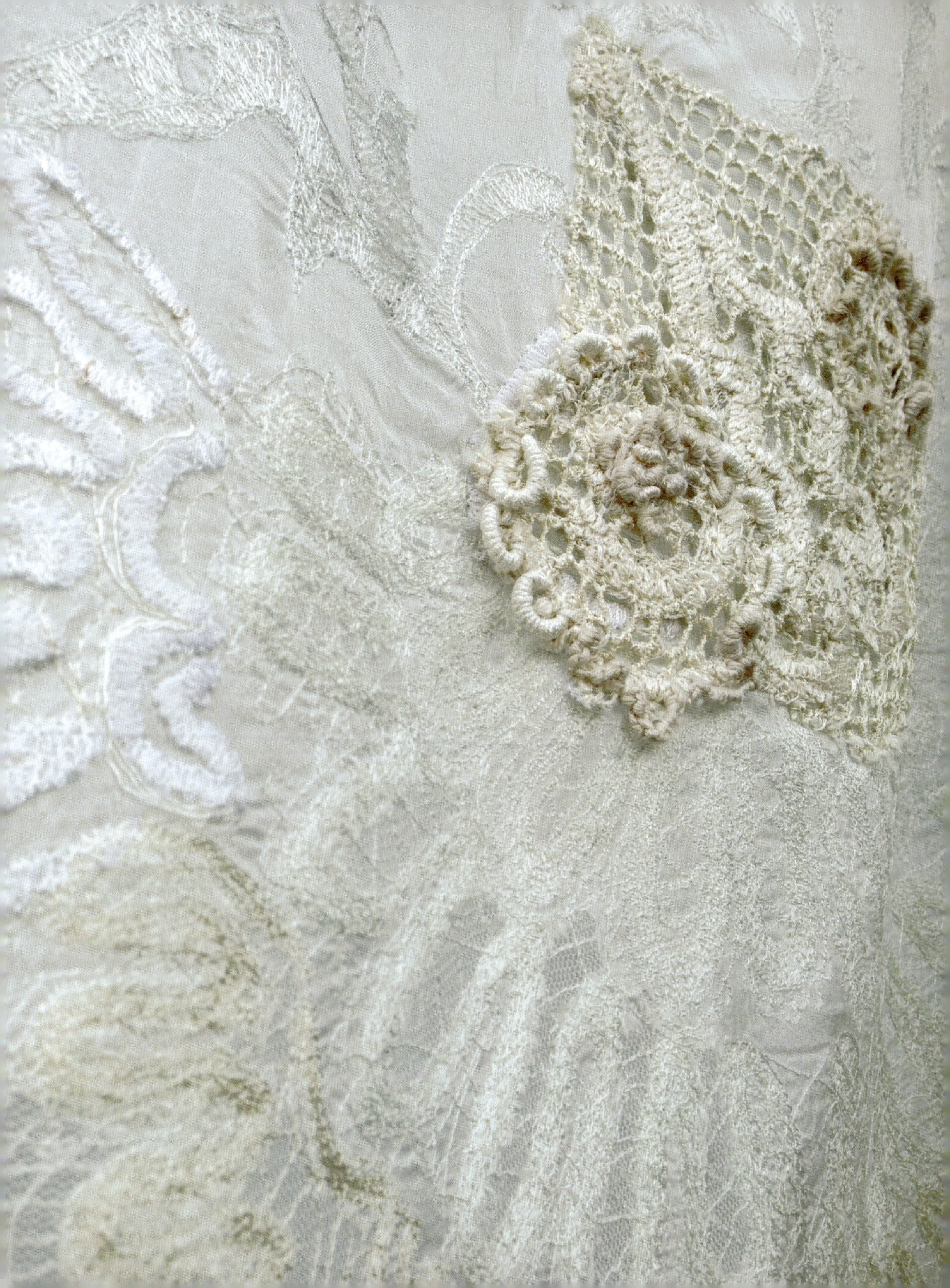

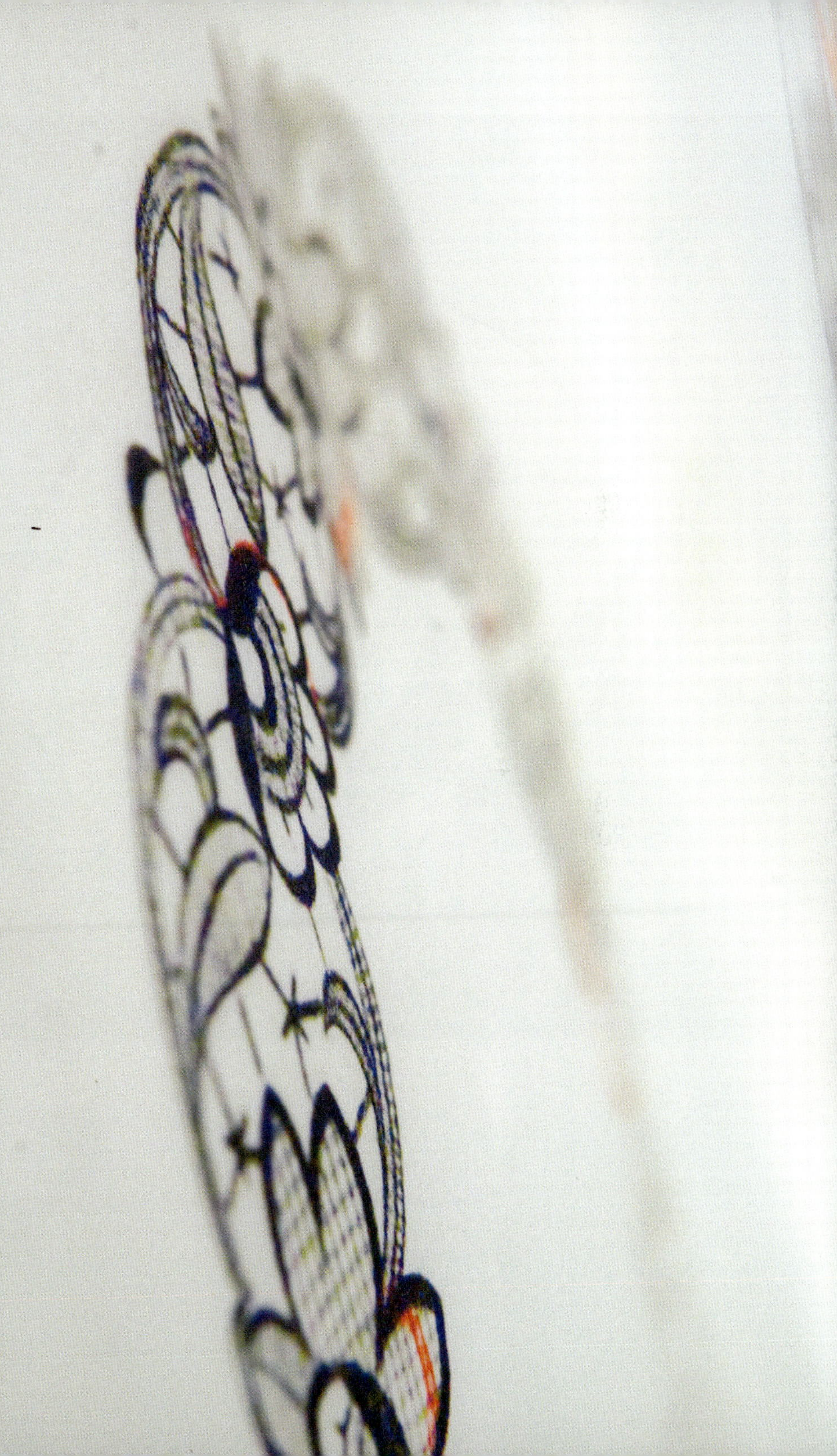

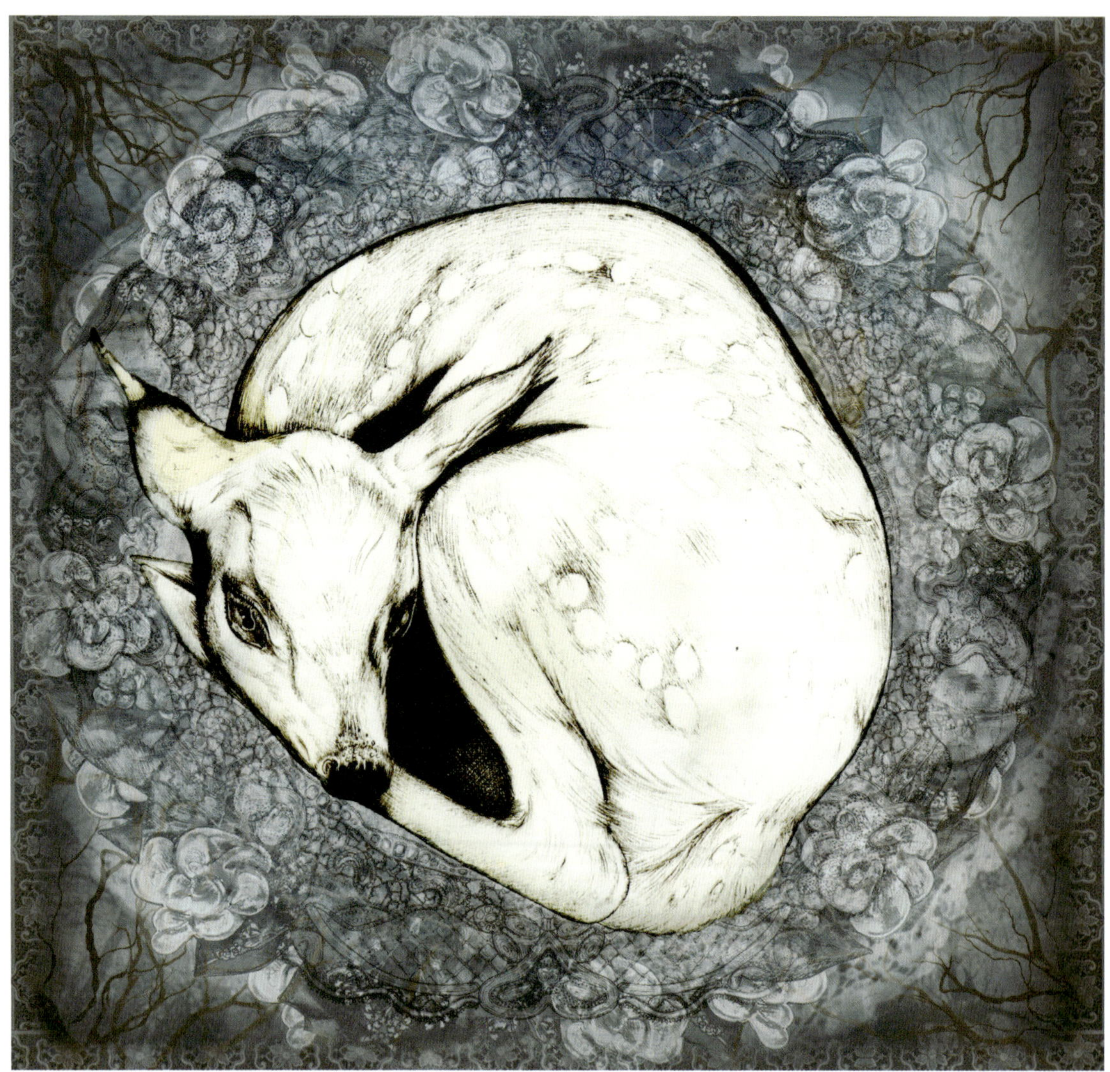

Louise Coleman
Inkjet print on silk viscose
velvet using reactive dyes.

Archive for future collaborations, student projects and possibilities. While handling and exploring these fabrics, portfolios and sample books, ideas flow fluidly. Later, through the process of developing the artworks, 'show and tell' events occurred where we could share and discuss our practice and engage with critical discussion. Individuals explored their ideas using a variety of materials, digital and technical processes as well as craft skills, through their personal inspirational imagery, textures, heritage and concepts that were conjured through the experience of venturing into the enclosed capsule that is the NTU Lace Archive. Digital print combined with screen printing and dévorè, hand, machine and digital embroidery and stitch, screen printing on paper, laser engraving on slate, as well as unusual combinations of materials such as metal and lace became processes through which the artists explored, reinterpreted and synthesised their ideas. Tessa Acti, a research assistant in the School, was inspired by the design portfolio of Verlag Von Christian Stoll as she felt that the unusual depiction of animals could capture her creative inquiry. This led her to explore the digital embroidery machine as a creative tool enabling her to develop a personal conversation with the technology.

Journeys in Lace—Part Two was exhibited in the Bonington Gallery, NTU. This exhibition demonstrated the creative interpretation by a selection of textiles, fashion and decorative art students of the Lace Archive. A selection of lace samples, around 20, was chosen from the Archive and was presented in a lecture format to the students to inspire their interest in using the Archive as part of their final second year project with the possibility of exhibiting in Journeys in Lace—Part Two. The students were then able to visit and look at more samples, as well as to learn more about lace design and why and how the Archive existed, putting this knowledge into the context of the city in which they were studying. They reported that this enriched their understanding of the Archive, of the School and art and design education. They also began to understand that the area they now spend time living and socialising within, the 'lace market', was once thriving, not with the bustle of contemporary urban living—warehouse style, or the buzz of bars and restaurants, but with the sounds of a workforce—manufacturing and exporting lace to a global market. The students explored 'lace' through various creative mediums, such as, drawing, material investigation, digital and hand printing, embroidery and for some the application or integration of these fabrics to fashion contexts through garments. Louise Coleman, then a second year undergraduate, used examples from the Archive that she found fascinating to draw. Her exceptional drawing skills were then used to 'weave' drawings of lace together with illustrative images of animals and rural scenes.

<u>Journeys in Lace—Part One</u>: Tessa Acti, Amanda Briggs-Goode, Maggie Bushby, Donna Carr, Kathy Dickinson, Debbie Gonet, Ottis Sturmey, Katherine Townsend, Sue Turton.
<u>Journeys in Lace—Part Two</u>: Chloe Blount, Jasmine Boden, Claire Bradshaw, Sarah Clifford, Louise Coleman, Serena Francis, Geri Li, Toni MacFarlane, Georgina Pearce, Natalie Raines, Sarah Patterson, Yashmin-Ul Siraj, Natalie Wilkins, Samantha Wing.

Lace Works: Contemporary Art and Nottingham Lace

Deborah Dean

Lace Works: Contemporary Art and Nottingham Lace took place at Nottingham Castle Museum & Art Gallery from 17 November 2012 to 10 February 2013. The exhibition curated by Dean had the Museum's founding vision at its heart. When it opened its doors to the public in 1878, the Museum unveiled a large 'lace gallery' and was also beginning to collect and display fine examples of Fine and Applied Art to inspire designers in the lace industry. Lace Works completed the circle, by using the samples acquired for the collection in these early years as a catalyst for new creativity. The exhibition included new commissions by Lucy Brown and Teresa Whitfield, who both drew ideas from the Museums' collection, alongside new work by Nicola Donovan and Joy Buttress, who took the Lace Archive at Nottingham Trent University (NTU) as a starting point. Existing work by Cal Lane and Timorous Beasties and items from the NTU Archive and Nottingham Museums' collection were also included to demonstrate a fascination with lace that goes beyond its traditional associations with lingerie, bridal wear and suburban window dressing.

This desire to reposition lace for contemporary audiences was of particular interest to Nicola Donovan, whose doctoral research helped to shape ideas for the exhibition in its early stages. Donovan devised a strategy for provoking dialogue about Nottingham lace and its history —essentially a series of 'field studies' during which she literally set out her stall of lace ideas and invited members of the public to share their stories with her. Her Lace Point stall appeared on Nottingham's Market Square during the Christmas Market in 2010. She also took it to Whitby Goth Weekend (November 2011) and Dark Materials at Tattershall Castle in Lincolnshire (2011); attended Asylum, a steampunk festival in Lincoln (2011); and made 'chocolace' at Nottingham's City Information Centre during the Light Night Festival in February 2012. The conversations triggered by these outings were rich and varied, encompassing both

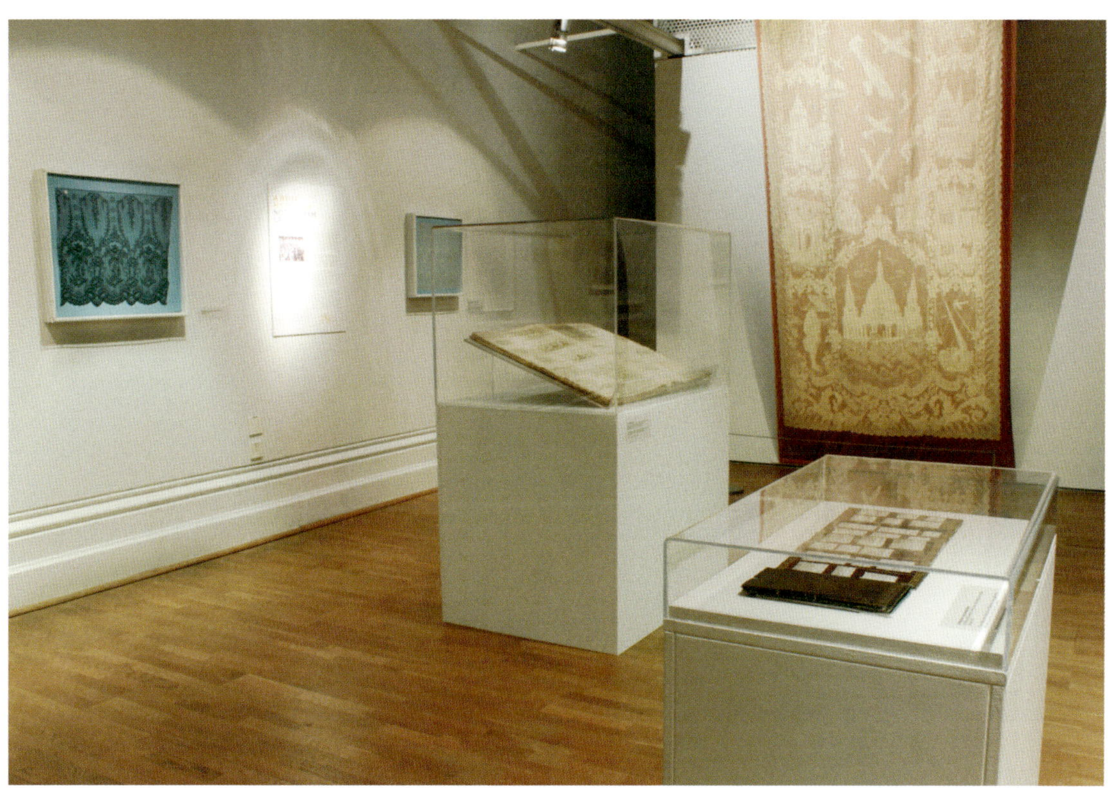

sadness and regret for the demise of a once great industry, and a desire to appropriate the language of lace to express allegiance to alternative, non-mainstream cultures.

Donovan's contribution to Lace Works was a distillation of these discussions and experimental forays in to the public realm. Her first piece, *Lacework,* 2011, was an audio recording of one of the last working Nottingham Leavers lace machines in the UK, made at Cluny Lace Co Ltd in Ilkeston. It was first staged in the Edwardian bandstand in the grounds of Nottingham Castle, 2011. Donovan said of the piece:

> To be in the presence of a working Leavers lace machine is a unique and exhilarating experience: the 'wall of sound' and rhythmic vibration that several tons of fine Victorian engineering produces, is reminiscent of a variety of stirring musical genres.[1]

Installation shot including the Battle of Britain lace panel, Leavers lace sample and lace pattern books. Courtesy Nottingham City Museums and Galleries, 2012. Photograph: David Severn.

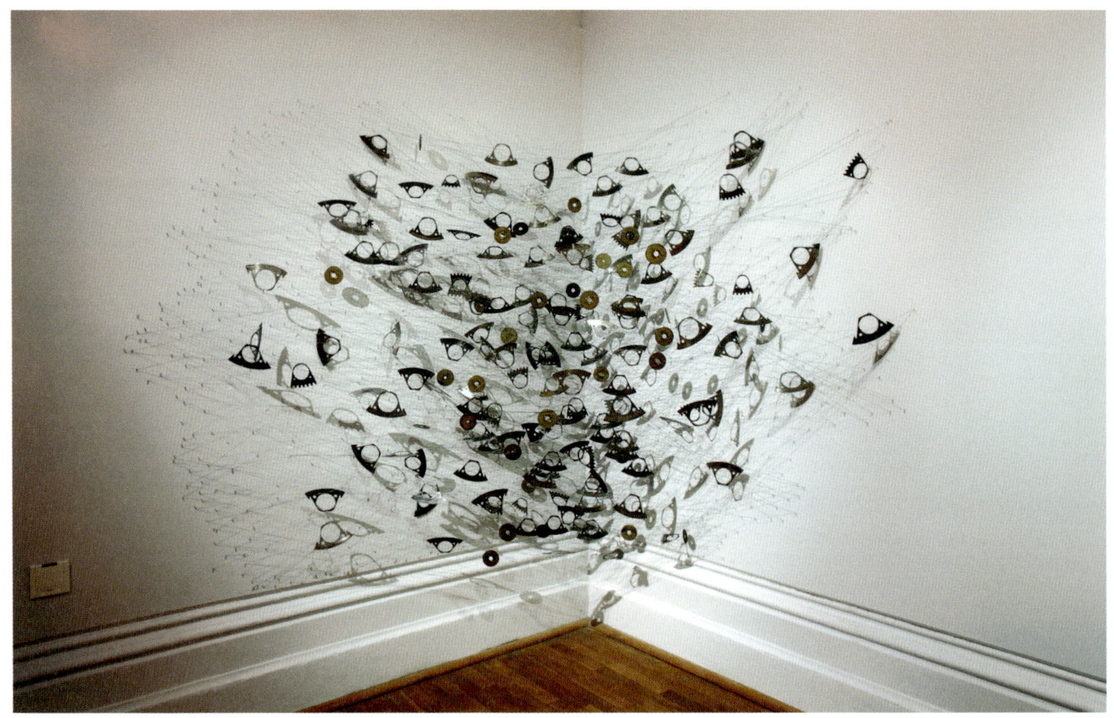

This interest in the disparity between heavy machinery and translucent fabric led the way to *Still*, 2012, a subtle installation, in which numerous metal lace carriages and bobbins were held in suspended animation by a web of fine threads, pinned to the walls. The metal parts were like quotations from the large machines to which they once belonged and yet were silenced and frozen in time and space. Their sharp edges held a latent threat, combined with a shimmering, jewel-like quality as they caught the light.

Bloom, 2012, emerged from an earlier series of paintings, in which Donovan embedded snippets of lace and pins into thick swathes of inky paint, with other uncommon bedfellows such as gas mask parts, animal bones and scalpel blades (*Bride*, *Hero* and *Siren*, all 2008). *Bloom* made use of Nottingham lace scraps and floral motifs, which Donovan grafted to the gallery walls as if lace was seeping from the fabric of the building. Inspired by mould patterns, the work hinted at meanings beyond the floral—the dusty bloom on a grape's skin or the milky deposit on the surface of an oil painting left in a damp room.

Nicola Donovan
Still
2012, thread, Nottingham lace machine
carriages and bobbins, dimensions variable.
Courtesy the Nottingham Trent University
Lace Archive.
Photograph: Marko Dukta.

Joy Buttress' work also demonstrates an interest in the ambiguities surrounding lace and our responses to it. For her, lace has the capacity to be both beautiful and repulsive, particularly when it becomes stained, brittle and discoloured with age. In earlier work developed from her doctorate research (*Lacuna*, 2012), she encrusted the soft white kidskin of vintage leather gloves with beads, iron filings, human hair, threads and wax. These lace-inspired embellishments appeared to grow from the leather and Buttress described how she was exploring:

> The notion that the decorative open-work structure of lace reveals the skin by exposing a boundary between our sensory body and the world around us, allowing for an intimate and shifting threshold.[2]

For her new piece, *Worn*, 2012, she used vintage French peasants' undergarments because they "embody and represent toil and hardship" and "are charged with the memories and traces of the women that wore them".[3] *Worn* exploited the distinction between utilitarian 'underwear' worn next to the skin for hygiene and protection, and lingerie with its suggestion of frivolity and sensuality. Digital and hand embroidery, glass beading, wax and gold foil were applied to the worn and patched cloth at the crotch and underarms of the garments, beautifying and drawing attention to those areas which are most likely to become marked and stained. The decoration was intricately detailed and yet—tantalisingly—it was applied to the inside of the garments, which in turn were suspended high up in the gallery space, almost out of reach. Buttress wanted "the viewer to be challenged to search for unseen and concealed interventions on the inner surface of the garments, suggesting intimacy, secrecy and suppression."[4]

Donovan and Buttress each produced work that provoked a certain 'double take' in the viewer; there was a contradiction at play, which is also present in the work of Cal Lane. Lane creates lace patterns in steel, often re-using existing objects such as the shovels and I-beam included in Lace Works and playing with the contrasts between the industrial and the fanciful, with transparency and solid form. A trained welder, she cuts the patterns herself and enjoys the way in which the work destabilises assumptions about materials and gender.

> I like to work as a visual devil's advocate, using contradiction as a way to create an empathetic image. By comparing and contrasting ideas and materials, my work creates a visual clash but also a sense of balance.[5]

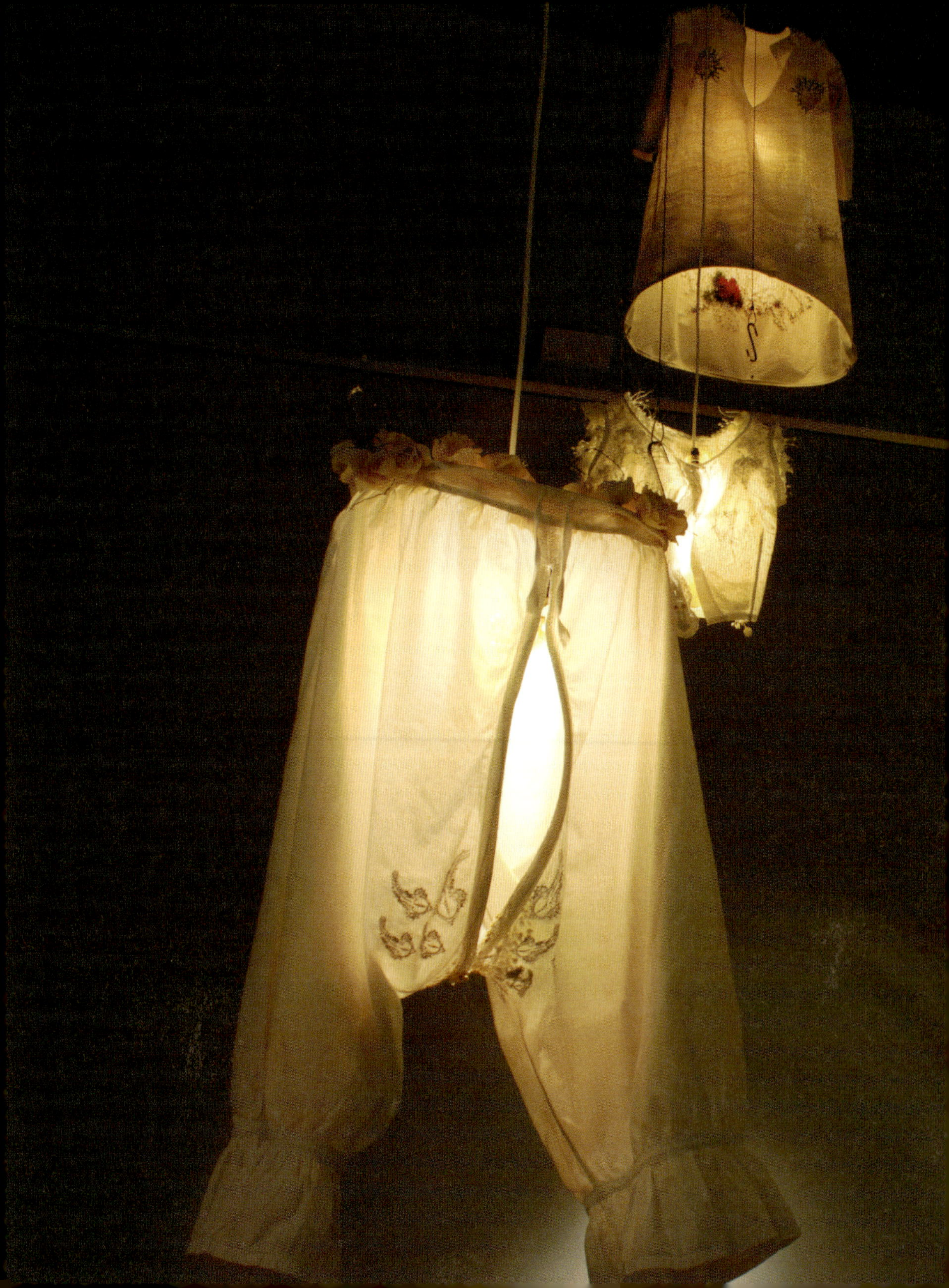

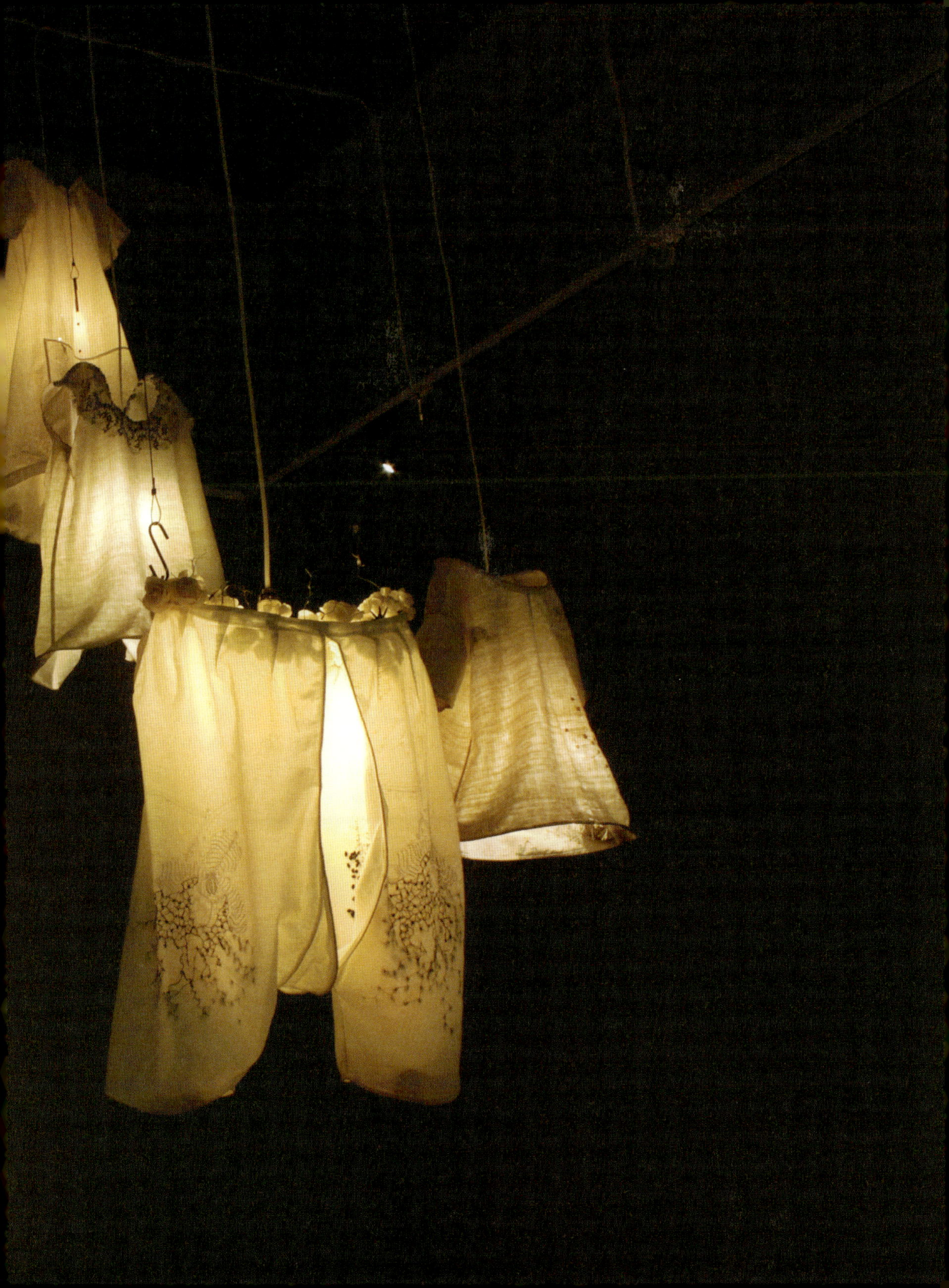

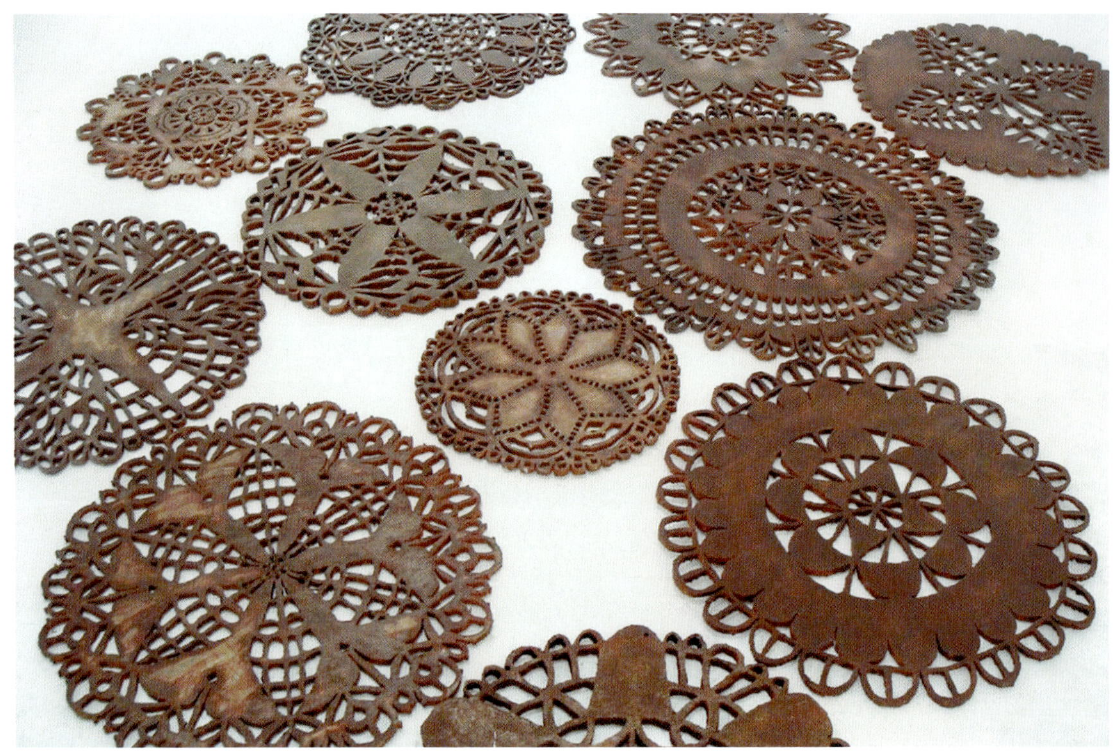

Three steel 'doilies' were also included in Lace Works, along with a 'rust print' made by laying one of the doilies on paper and leaving it in damp conditions until a rust impression of the pattern was left behind leaving a delicate, yet industrial, trace.

Over the past few years, Teresa Whitfield has made a series of life size drawings of hand-made lace and she was invited to make a new drawing of a piece of machine lace from Nottingham City Museums' collection for Lace Works. Whitfield's works have a startling hyper-reality to them and the new ink drawing (*Nottingham Machine Lace*, 2012) was exhibited side by side with the original piece of Leavers lace from c. 1910. An uncanny sense of *trompe l'oeil* was experienced as it became clear that what seemed to be fabric was in fact ink on paper; the drawing was more real than the object it depicted.

Another drawing by Whitfield—*Black Lace Shawl*, 2009—was shown on the wall of the Castle's grand South Hall staircase, alongside a piece of black *Devil Damask* machine lace draped theatrically down

Above
Cal Lane
Doilies
2002, oxyacetylene-cut steel
plates, dimensions variable.
Courtesy the artist and Art Mûr.

Opposite
Teresa Whitfield
Nottingham Machine Lace
2012, ink on paper, 78 x 66 cm.
Courtesy the artist, commissioned by Nottingham
Castle Museum and Art Gallery, with funding from the
Arts Council England through the National Lottery.

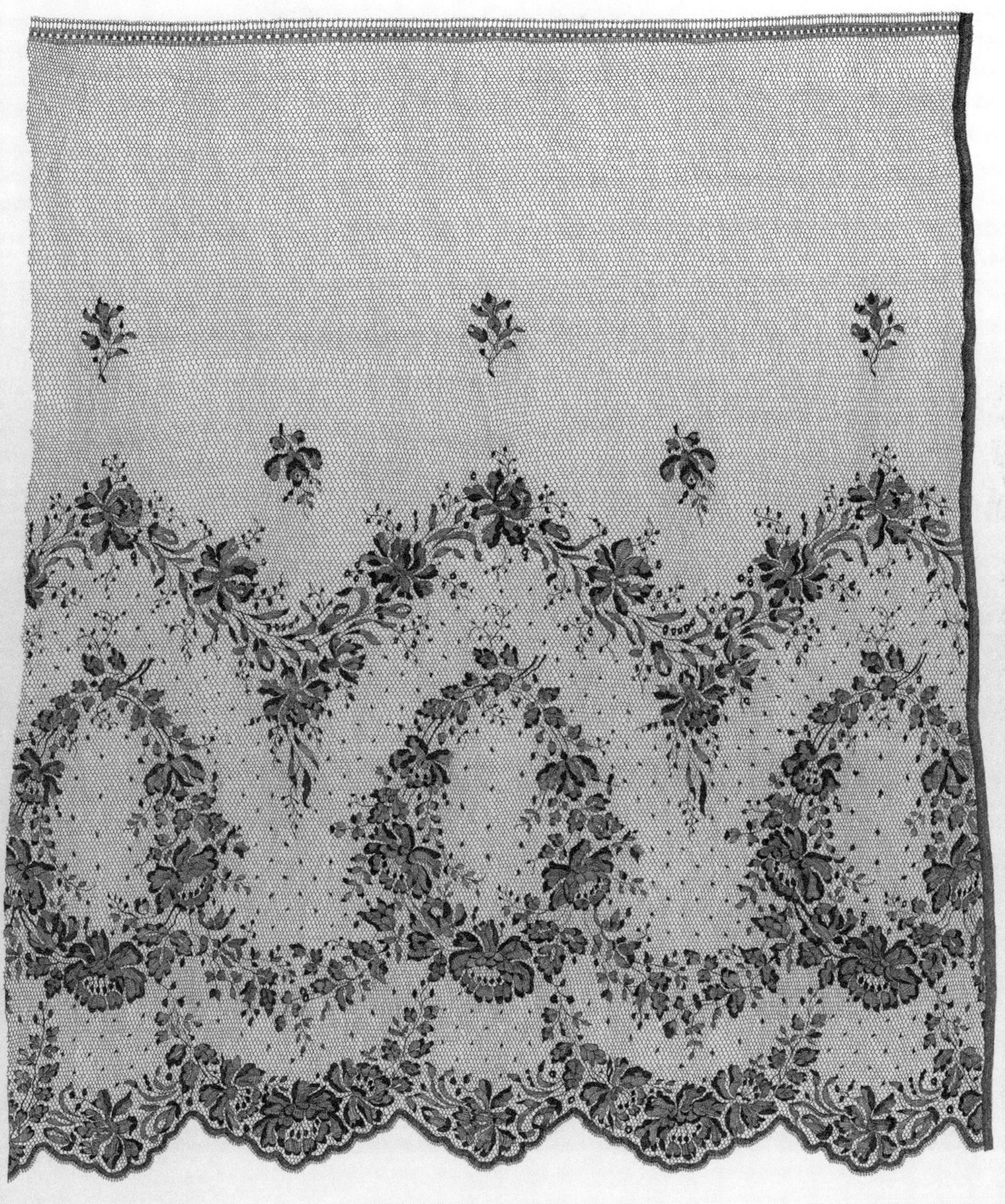

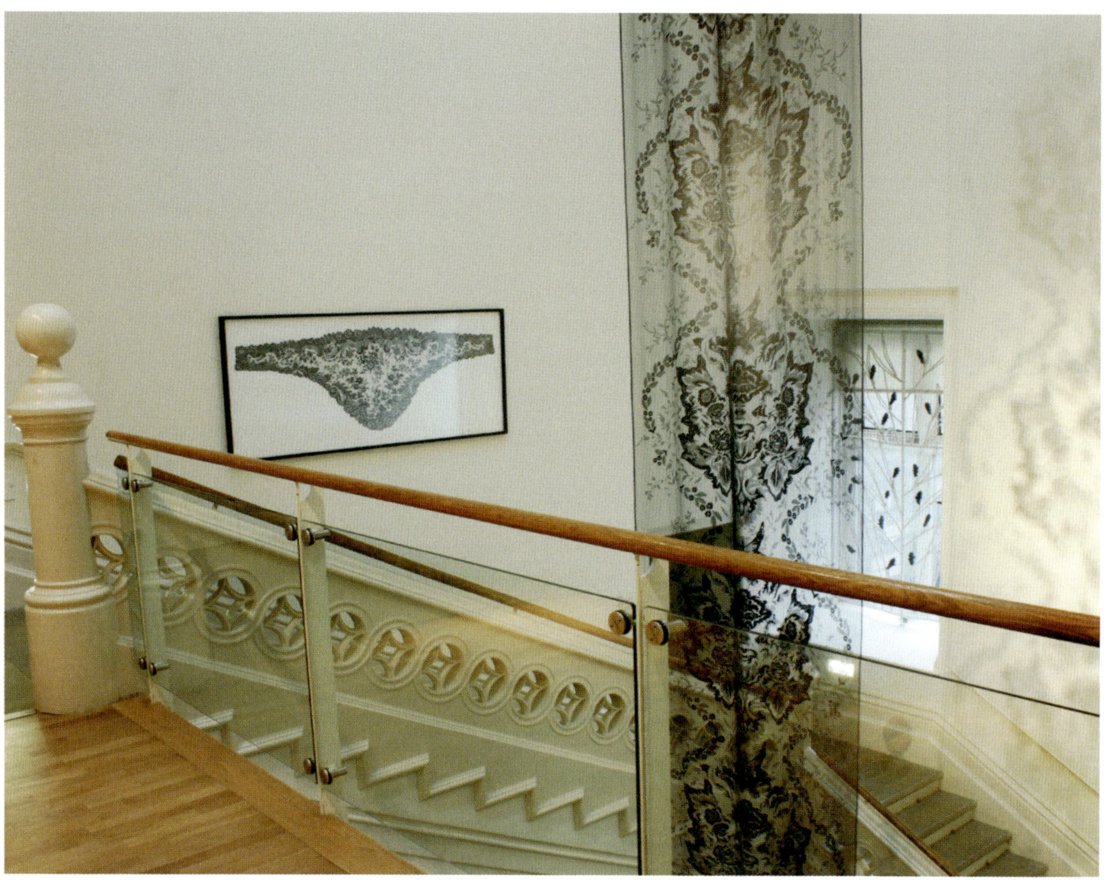

the full 16 metre drop of the stairwell. This lace was designed by Timorous Beasties, well-known for their surreal and provocative textiles and wallpaper designs, and produced on a Nottingham Leavers lace machine by Morton Young and Borland Ltd in Newmilns, Ayrshire, Scotland. In their hands, the traditional and familiar turns out to have a darker side and this is typified by *Devil Damask*. Hidden at first sight within the floral swags and foliage of the length of curtain lace, a devil's face emerges as the eye adjusts and the viewer is left with the unsettling sense of a Rorschach inkblot test.

The exhibition also included *The Battle of Britain Lace Panel* (c. 1943–46), a piece of Ecru machine-made curtain lace, designed by Harry Cross and manufactured by Dobson, Browne & Co, Delbeta House, Queens

Installation view:
Timorous Beasties
Devil Damask;
Teresa Whitfield.
Black Lace Shawl
2012, dimensions variable.
Photograph: David Severn.

Road, Nottingham to commemorate the Battle of Britain, 1940. This piece amply demonstrates that lace designers could turn their hand to a wide range of subjects and historical events, however incongruous the subject matter.

The manufacture of wide runs of machine lace suitable for window coverings was made possible by the invention of the lace curtain machine by John Livesey in Nottingham in 1846. The lace curtain became ubiquitous as a marker of taste and class status in the late-nineteenth and early-twentieth century. Carol Quarini has observed that:

> Like the domestic, the net curtain is concerned with boundaries and their unstable, permeable nature. In its uncanny guise as domestic veil, the net curtain reflects the duality of the transparent domestic boundary and reveals as much as it conceals.[6]

Lucy Brown drew on these associations for *Veil*, her temporary outdoor installation made for the colonnade outside the main entrance to the Castle building. The colonnade is home to a group of bronze and marble portrait busts of writers and poets associated with Nottingham, including Lord Byron and DH Lawrence. Brown shrouded three of these portrait heads in lace curtain fabric, securing the folds with cord which she bound belt-like around each sculptural form. Like dustsheets thrown over furniture in an unoccupied country house, the net formed a protective boundary and yet Brown allowed the viewer to peep underneath, cutting away some of the lace to reveal details such as the face of Mary Howitt—the only woman amongst the sculpted writers.

Veil developed from an earlier work *Wrapping of the Jaipur Gate*, 2009, outside Hove Museum & Art Gallery. For Brown, "the act of wrapping is a ritual, whether the intention is to preserve, protect or to conceal".[7] In her wider practice, she has been using second-hand clothes in her work for some time, wearing them first to get a sense of their history, before deconstructing and re-weaving them in to new and 'unwearable' garments. More recently, she has stopped short of making 'stand alone' garments and instead cut the work loose from its loom, allowing it to spread its tendrils across the gallery space.

The secrets we keep from ourselves was made in this way and emerged from Brown's research visits to Nottingham Museums' lace collection. It incorporated hand-dyed Nottingham Leavers lace (manufactured by Douglas Gill), ribbon and garments sourced from charity shops, eBay and the artist's own wardrobe. It reflected the artist's interest in photographs of female lace workers, which typically

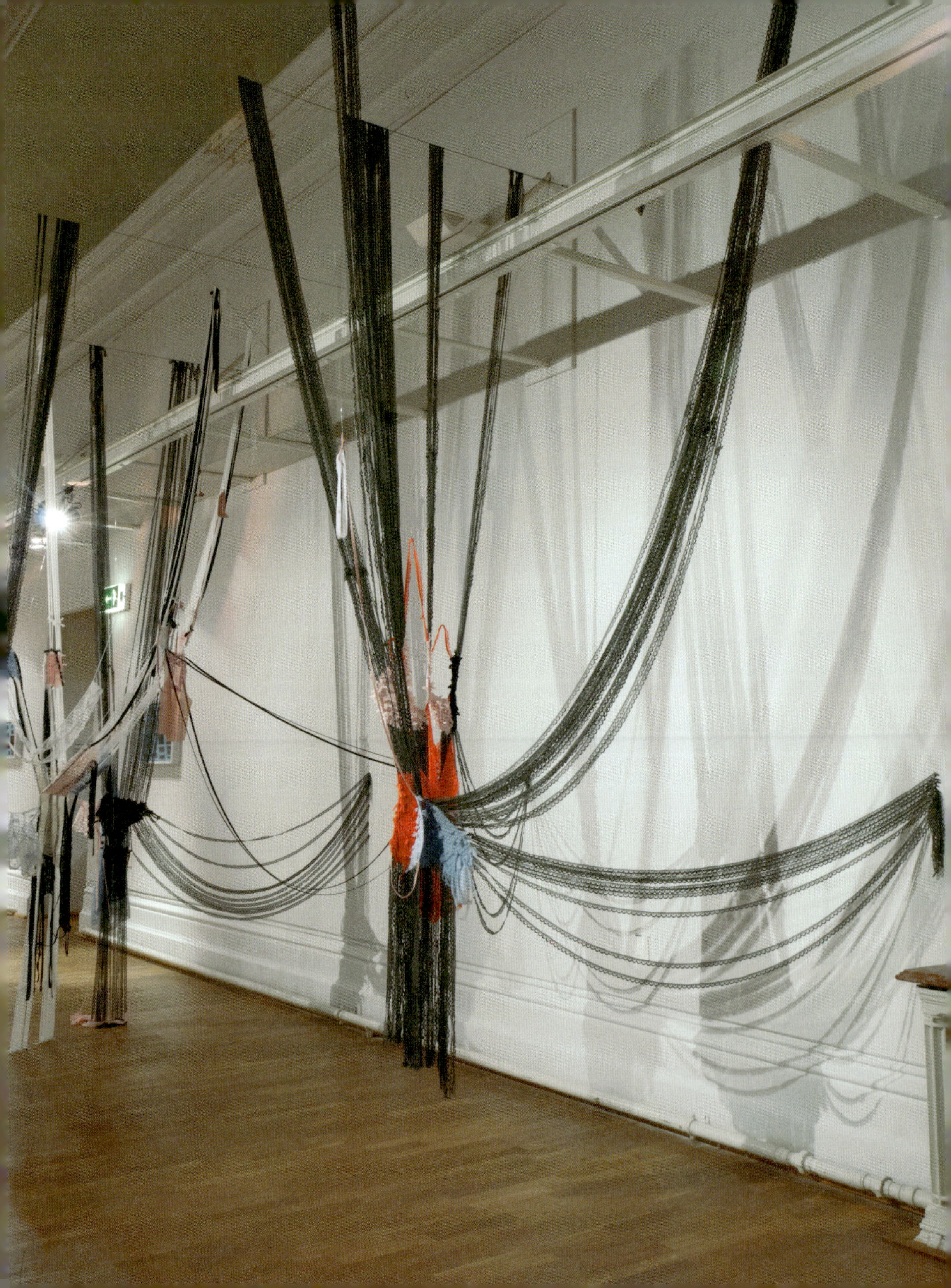

show women sitting close together, each checking and mending flaws in the lace. Brown was struck by how this activity remained virtually the same over the decades and how the lace was "a physical point of connection between the women, their hands moving thread and fabric, heads bent, skirts touching".[8]

The piece also explored Brown's interest in the semi-transparent qualities of lace and the way in which it conceals and reveals at the same time. The weaving therefore incorporated lace lingerie, both whole garments trapped in the warp and weft, and re-woven fragments that retained only a hint of their former life.

Installed in the gallery, all these elements were connected by the lace ribbon and suspended in space like trapeze artists caught in mid-flight. The 'performative' quality of these looping forms seemed to hold a memory of the artist's movements, as if she had been threading a giant lace machine ready for production

Over 23,000 people saw Lace Works and the exhibition demonstrated artists' fascination with historical lace, as well as the enormous potential of Nottingham City Museums and Galleries' collection to trigger excitement, engagement and new creativity. The partnership with Nottingham Trent University to deliver the lace:here:now project has allowed the Museums Service to revisit its collection from a new perspective, make it visible to a much wider public and work together as a city to place Nottingham's internationally important lace heritage back on the map where it belongs.

1. Nicola Donovan, notes for Lace Works, 2011.
2. Joy Buttress via email 2012.
3. Joy Butress, email conversation with Deborah Dean, 2012.
4. Joy Butress, email conversation with Deborah Dean, 2012.
5. Cal Lane, artist's website.
6. Carol Quarini, *The Transparent Domestic Boundary*, Lost in Lace exhibition catalogue, edited by Lesley Millar, published by Birmingham Museum & Art Gallery, 2011.
7. Lucy Brown, Axis website.
8. Lucy Brown, email conversation with Deborah Dean.

Lucy Brown
<u>The secrets we keep from ourselves</u>
2012, hand-dyed Nottingham Leavers lace (manufactured by Douglas Gill), ribbon, vintage garments sourced from charity shops, eBay and the artist's own wardrobe, dimensions variable.
Photograph: John Hartley.

Case study I
Timorous Beasties

<u>Name</u> Paul Simmons.

<u>Occupation</u> Co-founder of design studio Timorous Beasties.

<u>Short Biography</u> Noted for surreal and provocative textiles and wallpapers, the design studio, Timorous Beasties, was founded in Glasgow in 1990 by Alistair McAuley and Paul Simmons, who met studying Textile Design at the Glasgow School of Art. Winners of the Walpole Award for "Best Emerging British Luxury Brand" in 2007 and "British Luxury Design Talent" in 2010, they have branded showrooms in London and Glasgow, and export their luxury products and design worldwide.

<u>Exhibitions/Shows/Commissions/Collaborations</u> Barkli Park.

<u>Client</u> Yoo.

<u>Date</u> February 2012.

<u>Project Background</u> Timorous Beasties were commissioned by Yoo to design Nottingham Lace drapes for the public area of Barkli Park, a development of 130 luxury apartments in Central Moscow. The Silver Birch lace was specially designed to make the most of the six metre drops and reflect the 'nature' theme carried throughout the development. Barkli Park is the first Yoo inspired by Philippe Starck project in Russia, located in the heart of Moscow next to Ekaterininskiy Park.

When did lace designs become a part of your practice and what was the motivation behind this?
As a company we aim to create challenging and dynamic conversational designs in the high-end wallpaper and interior fabric markets and

have always wanted to counter the 'twee' image of textiles. We have an experimental approach and invest in new design techniques which allows us to move into a range of other product areas such as lace, jacquards, lighting, rugs and ceramics. We began working with lace in 2005 as part of a commission for the Wellcome Trust. This project was intended to show the benefits and impact of the Wellcome Trust and so for the backdrop for the show we decided to produce Nottingham Lace, inspired by the first line of defence against malaria—the mosquito net—delicately woven with mosquitos, syringes and microscopes.

How did you relationship with lace manufacturers Morton Young and Borland Ltd (MYB) start?
We first made contact with MYB through this initial commission and through the process of developing the lace for the Wellcome Trust. We realised that this process offered us masses of potential and we wanted to experiment with it further. We now have nine Nottingham Lace designs in our collection.

Can you tell us about the development process that led you developing lace designs?
We enjoy diversifying, and designing for Nottingham Lace appeared to be a challenging course, but also the time felt right to invigorate this textile process. The challenges came through the fact that the image is not built in a traditional way. We needed to think about lines of threads twisting and turning, and how to connect the image, with holes being as important as the 'solid' areas, and tonal density being vital to the development of the design. But we find technical constraints both challenging and enjoy pitting our creativity against those obstacles. We design with the production problems in view. We have a massive interest in history, and I collect all sorts of things: ceramics, silhouette portraits, prints, books, woodblocks and books on natural history. For us drawing is an extraordinarily important process and to be a good designer you need to put in the time to draw. I work mainly on the computer at the design development stages, but it is important to maintain control over the whole working process. This involves drawing, often with pen and inks, scanning, printing, re-working and scanning again. In addition, developing the designs tonally helps to advance the progression of lace designs.

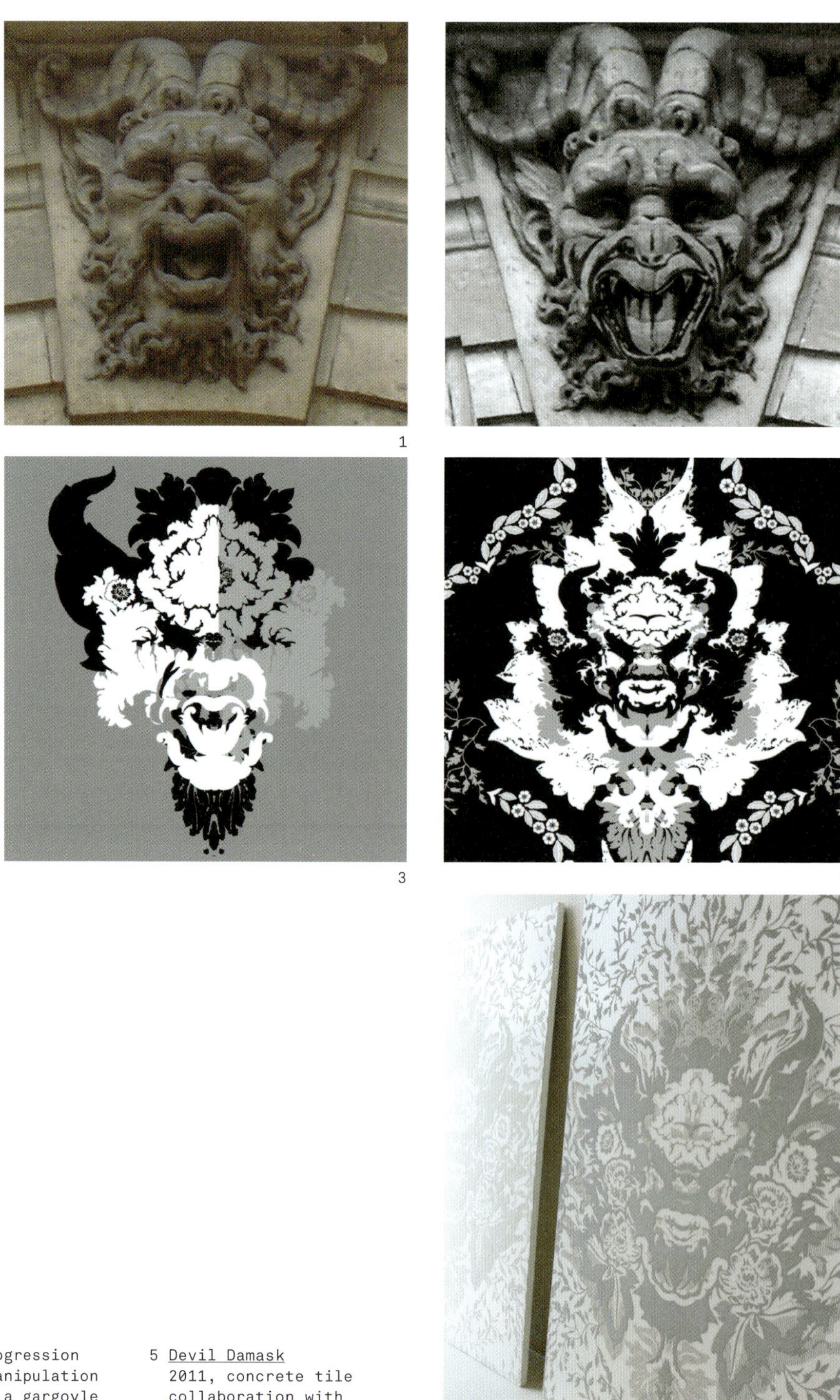

1-4: Design progression
 and digital manipulation
 from image of a gargoyle
 to lace design.

5 <u>Devil Damask</u>
 2011, concrete tile
 collaboration with
 Graphic Relief.

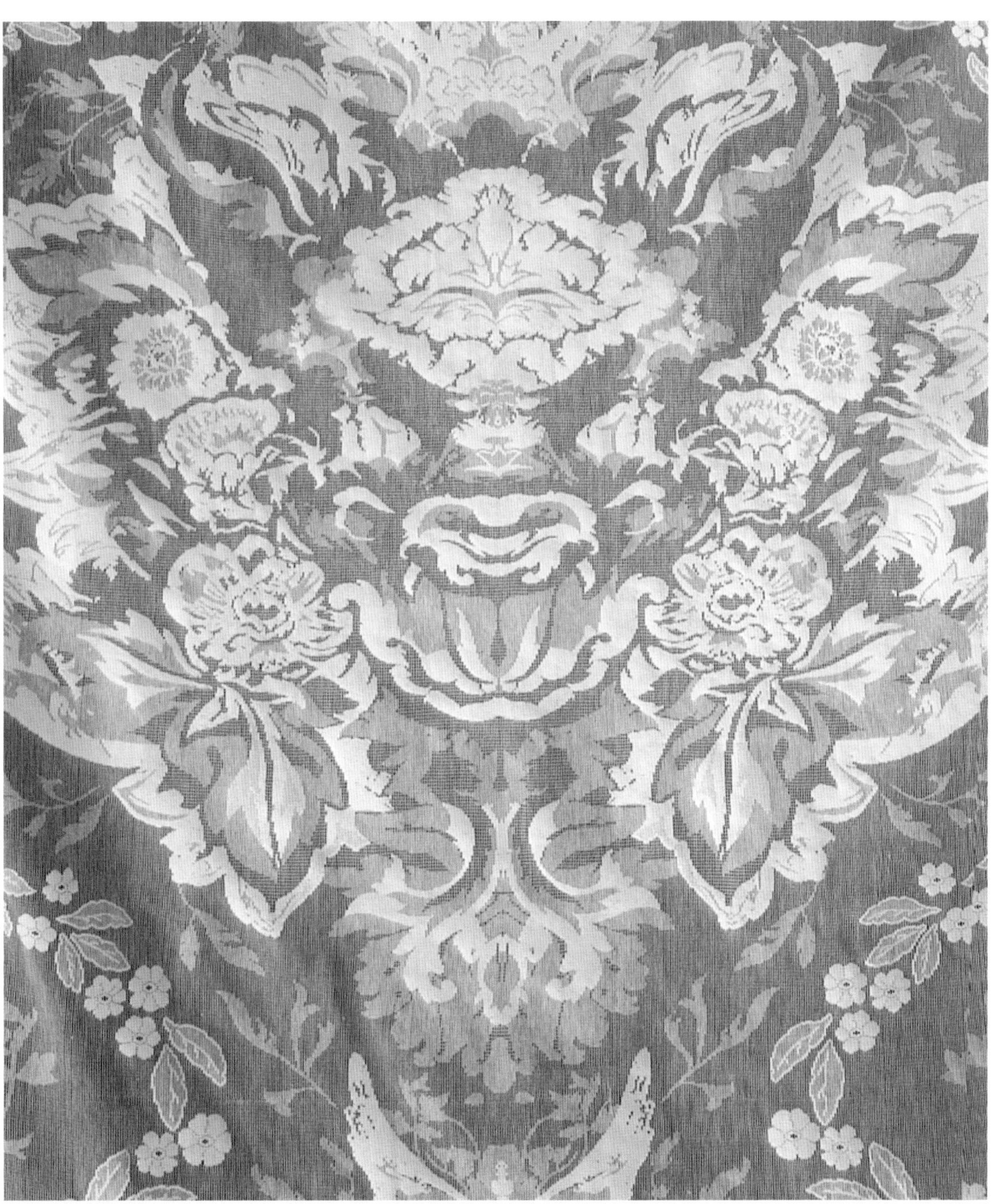

<u>Devil Damask</u>
2011, concrete tile
collaboration with
Graphic Relief.

Case study II
Cecilia Heffer

<u>Name</u> Cecilia Heffer.

<u>Short Biography</u> Cecilia Heffer is a practice-based researcher, textile designer, lecturer and curator who specialises in contemporary lace and textile innovation. Her research specifically explores the integration of the hand-made with emerging technologies. Her focus is to investigate contemporary translations of lace as a vehicle for innovative textile design concepts.

<u>2013</u> Fourteenth International Tapestry Triennial, Central Museum of Textiles, Lodz Poland.

<u>2012–2013</u> Negotiating this world: Contemporary Australian Art, The Ian Potter Centre: National Gallery of Victoria Australia, group show.

<u>2011–2013</u> Love Lace, Powerhouse Museum International Lace Award.

<u>2012</u> Seventh International Fibre Art Biennale Exhibition, Beijing, China, group show.

In 2005, while I was researching for a solo exhibition, I discovered the Lace Study Centre at the Powerhouse Museum Sydney. It houses a Lace collection of over 200 pieces and is well known for the volunteers who demonstrate how to create Bobbin Lace. I became acquainted with Lace Historian Rosemary Sheperd and through a series of workshops, I attempted to learn traditional bobbin lacemaking. The process was very much a starting point. However it was through this haptic engagement that I gained a deeper understanding of Sheperd's definition of lace as an ″open work surface where the pattern of spaces are as important as the solid motif″.

This definition has been my guiding principle that I still approach my practice in contemporary lace today.

Through working in lace archives I have been influenced and fascinated by human innovation. The question always begs to be asked, how did they make that? Whether analysing a hand-made lace or a machine lace, the extraordinary complexity of pattern and structure, beauty and mastery of technique is a constant source of inspiration. Consequently in my practice, I try and hint at an historical lineage, translating past traditions in a visual and material language that is relevant to this day and age. I aim to integrate the hand-made with new technologies. It is in this new space, the intersection of the two that new work is created.

Other lace archives that have influenced me include the extensive lace collection at Nottingham Trent University (NTU). I was fortunate enough to view the collection and this experience has initiated my interest in machine-made laces, their processes and historical methods of recording lace on photographic paper.

The commission to design the lace curtains for Government House also introduced me to the company Morton Young and Borland Ltd in Scotland. On a visit to the studio I was shown their lace archives of original hand painted lace designs. Their loom is the widest in the world, linked to a CAD system it is a working example of hand and technology.

The duality of lace inspires me. At first you are drawn to the beauty of its surface and then intrigued by the magic and transparency of its ephemeral nature. It is a textile that has a rich and cultural past with stories to tell. It plays with the notion of positive and negative space and captivates through its shadow and ethereality. The shadow that lace creates adds a layer of meaning to the work.

Could you tell us more about your award winning artwork Inter-Lace *for the Love Lace exhibition at the Powerhouse Museum, Sydney?*
Inter-lace is an interactive digital lace installation and was a collaboration research project with a colleague, Associate Professor of Interactive Design, Bert Bongers, from the University of Technology Sydney.

Designed as a visual, spatial and tangible sensory experience, the installation transformed lace into a three-dimensional augmented environment. Traditional expressions of lace pattern were redefined through the use of innovative materials, process and video technologies.

Sensors were stitched into fragile delicate lace surfaces and were designed to detect changes in light, proximity and movement of

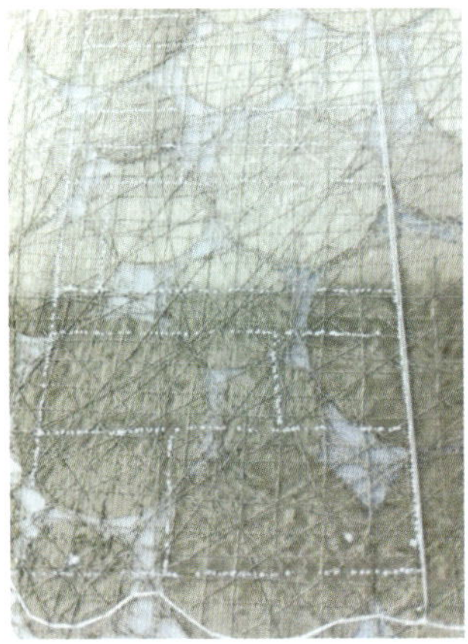

1

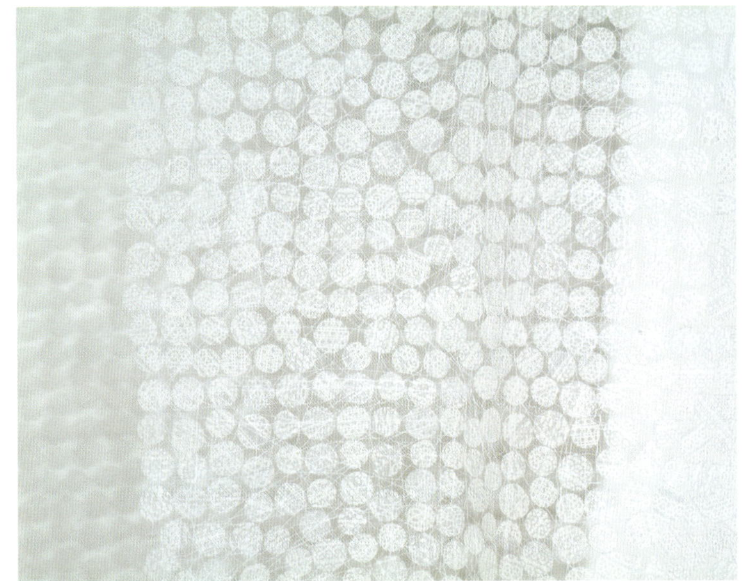

2

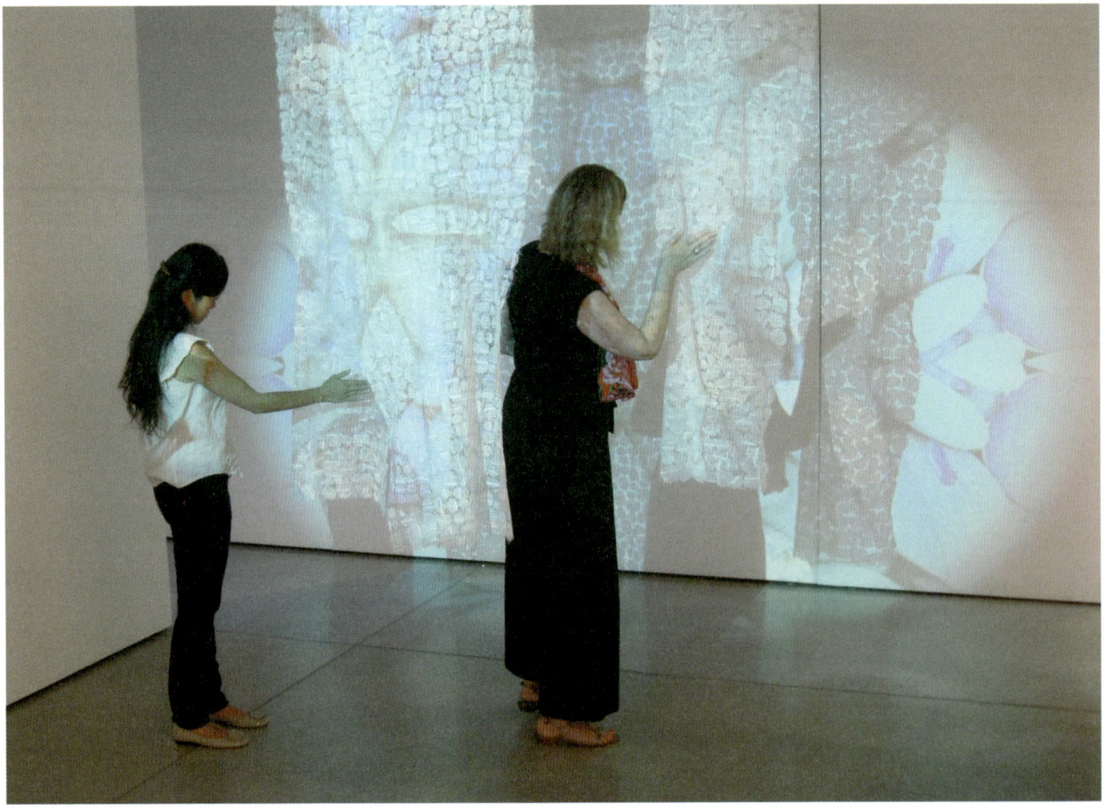

3

audience. Through experimentation it was discovered that the sensors responded to each other consequently and the light projections were in constant flux. The installation enabled the audience to explore the spatial mysterious interplay between real and virtual worlds. Its layers explored light and shadow between material and ephemeral perceptions of space.

Future projects will look at how lace can extend our perception and relationship to pattern and space and in doing so potentially shift the way people experience their environment. I aim to answer the following questions: how can a lace scape be designed to provide a space, a window of contemplation, an ethereal escape or a moment to imagine? And could these have future implications for wellbeing and healthcare?

1 <u>India Embroidery Lace</u> series
  2013, silk shantung,
  eucalyptus and natural tea
  dyes, traditional Indian
  Long Embroidery stitch,
  30 x 30 cm.
  Photograph: Cecilia Heffer.

2 <u>Reticella Lace</u>
  2006, silk shantung, hand
  printed Venetian Lace braid
  patterns, stitched onto a
  soluble substrate,
  170 x 65 cm.
  Photograph: Paul Pavlou.

3 <u>Inter-Lace</u>
  2011–2013, silk organza,
  silk screen printed,
  sensors, video projection,
  three lace panels,
  180 x 70 cm.
  Photograph: Bert Bongers.

4 <u>Inter-Lace</u> (detail)
  2011–2013.

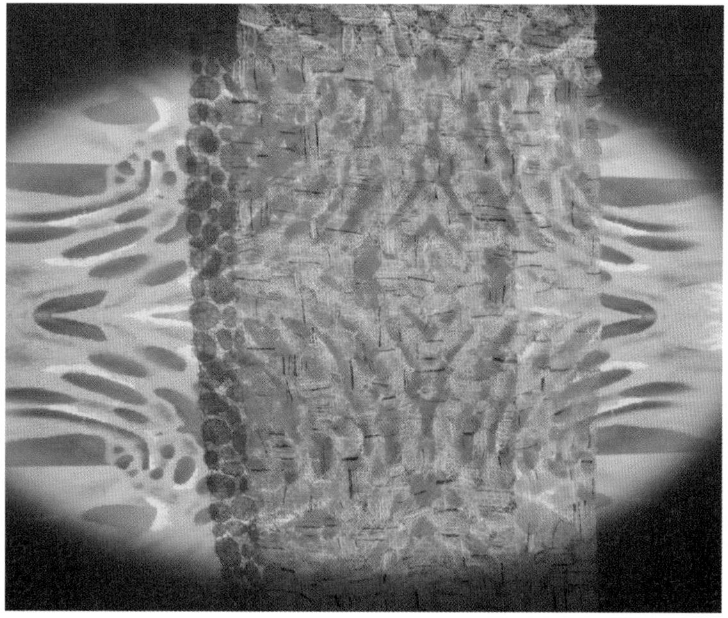

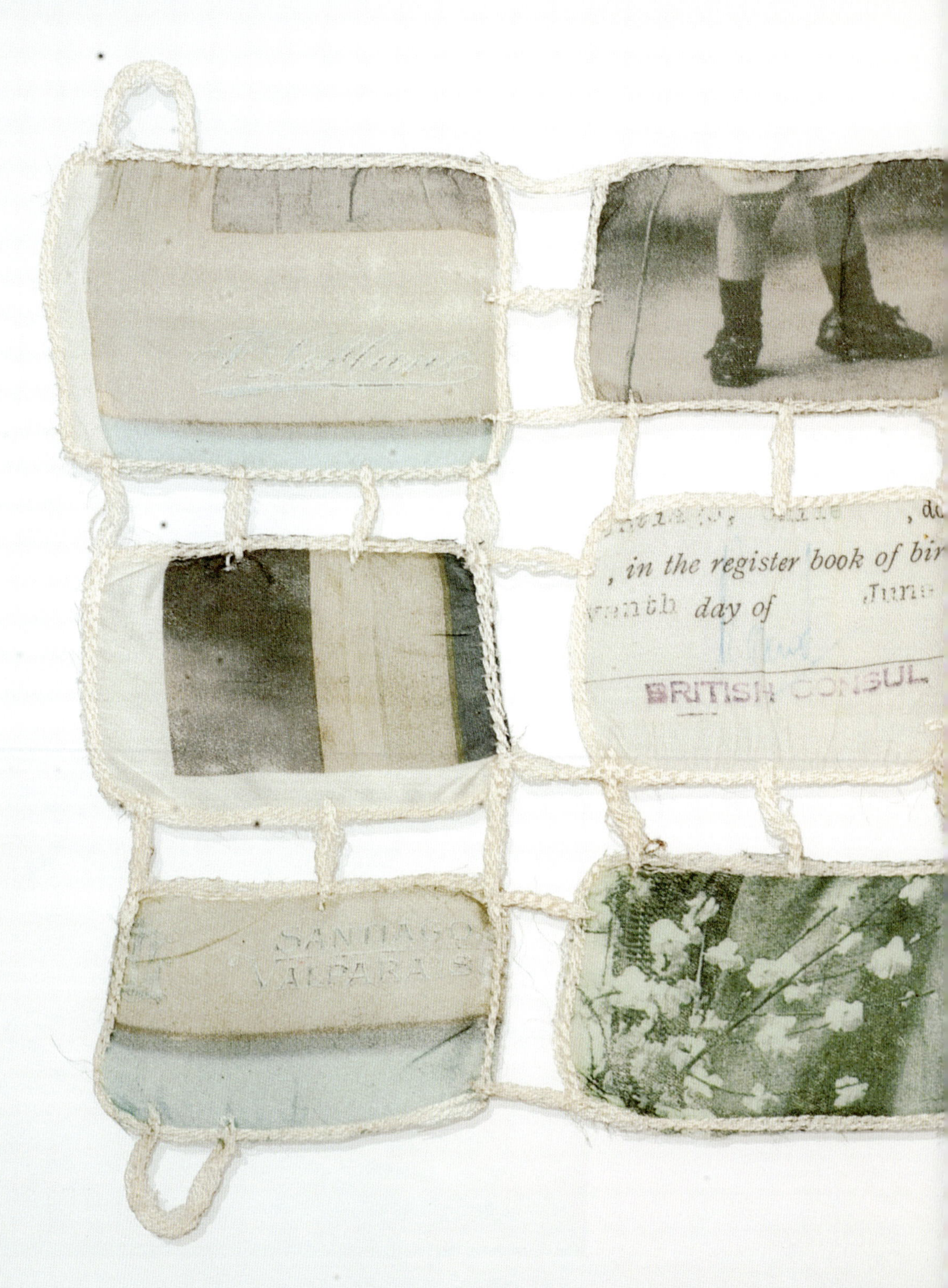
in the register book of bir
day of   June
BRITISH CONSUL
SANTIAGO
VALPARA

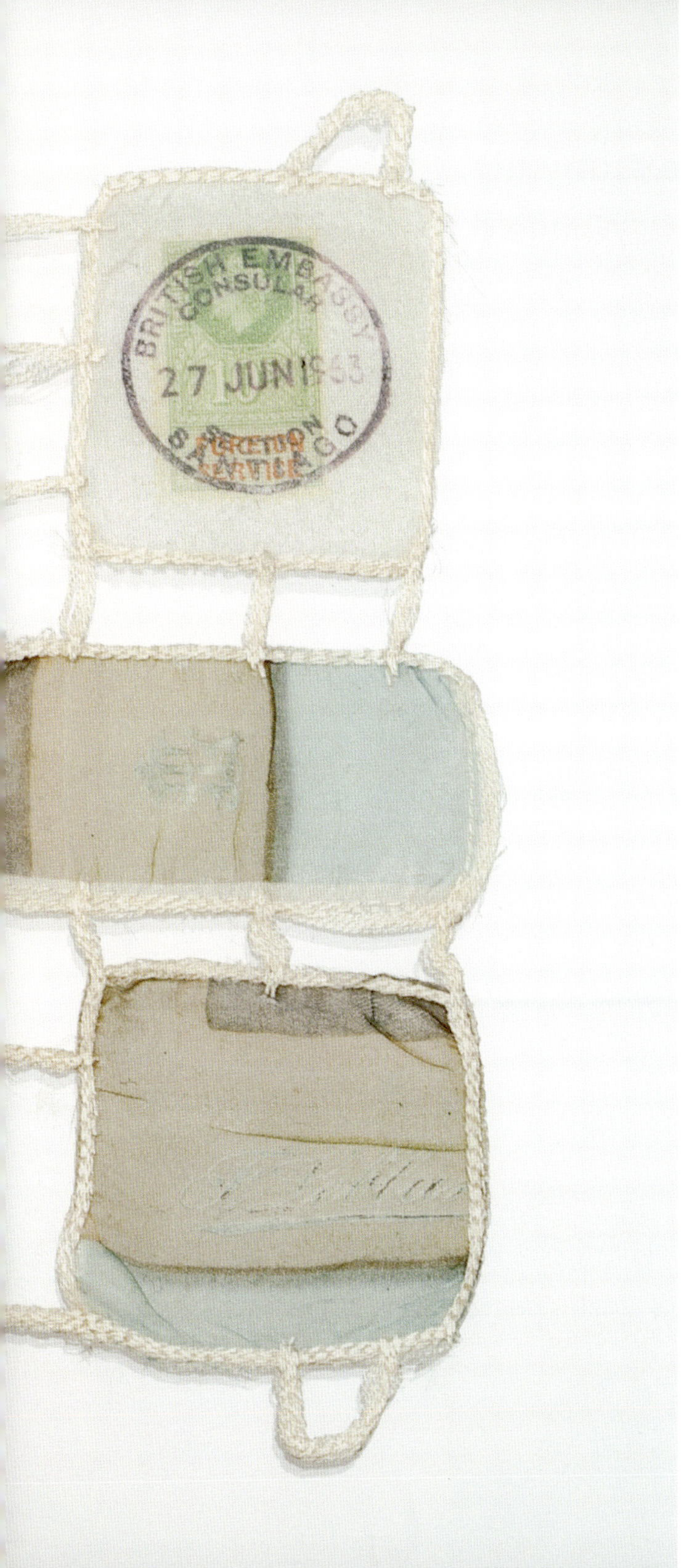

Lace Narratives series
2012, transfer photo, silk
satin organza, machine
stitching, 18 x 15 cm.
Photograph: Paul Pavlou.

Case study III
Teresa Whitfield

<u>Name</u> Teresa Whitfield.

<u>Short Biography</u> Teresa Whitfield photographs and draws antique lace from archives including the V&A Museum, Bronte Parsonage Museum and the Fashion Museum in Bath. In the drawings, items of lace are painstakingly reconstructed in black or white ink, an activity which both negates technology and embraces the imperfections inherent in the hand-made objects to which the drawings refer. I am interested in exploring what the lacemaking process tells us about the social history of women; as well as exploring the solitary lacemaker I have also made work which explores the tradition of lacemaking by large groups of women.

<u>Solo exhibitions</u>
<u>2009</u> Drawing Lace, Worthing Museum & Art Gallery, Worthing, West Sussex
<u>2008</u> Drawing Lace, Thelma Hulbert Gallery, Honiton, Devon

<u>Group exhibitions</u>
<u>2012</u> Wildness Between the Lines, Leeds College of Art, Leeds
<u>2012</u> Lace Works: Contemporary Art & Nottingham Lace, Nottingham Castle Museum & Art Gallery, Nottingham
<u>2009</u> Jerwood Drawing Prize, Jerwood Space, London

Why did lace become the source of inspiration for your artworks?
My fascination with lace was instigated by the recognition of a close similarity between lace and line drawing. In early hand-made lace, such as Honiton lace, the threads which have been woven in miniature by the use of bobbins are all entirely visible on a flat two-dimensional surface exactly like line drawing. Unlike other textiles such as

embroidery where the threads are overlaid in a similar way to darning, in lace the journey of each individual strand can be followed by the eye and can therefore be easily translated into a drawn line. I am really passionate about drawing and have focussed my entire practice as an artist on drawing for the last 15 years; when I discovered lace in a small encyclopedia of needlework I was compelled to translate it into drawing.

Can you tell us about your intricate drawing process and what happens if you make a mistake?
The technique that I use has evolved in tandem with my interest in lace and has developed from what started as a semi-abstract depiction of woven surfaces to a more forensic examination of the precise techniques utilised in specific items of historically important lace. The level of realism in my work often confuses the viewer as to whether they are contemplating a real piece of lace or a photograph; the drawings occupy an unusual space between the drawing of an object and the recreation of it in a different medium.

The drawing method that I use is very similar to the process of using thread and so the drawings are more like a reenactment of needle-work than simply a likeness to the end product. During a residency at Fabrica in Brighton I worked with a team of assistants over a six week period to draw a large black lace shawl in a reenactment of the communal lacemaking process which was inspired by the 200 Honiton lacemakers who took six months to make Queen Victoria's wedding dress.

In order to achieve the high level of detail characteristic of lace, I use very fine Rotring pens and ink; the lace is firstly photographed and printed out life-size for reference during the drawing. I work in layers, starting with the basic weave of the design before moving on to more detailed elements such as the background netting. Ironically, any small errors that occur can add a greater sense of realism where tiny threads appear to intersect each other, recording the miniscule defects in the fabric and the way the threads naturally interweave. But more usually mistakes are just not visible because they are occurring on such a small scale.

How important is it that the artworks are all completed by hand?
There has been a resurgence of interest in the cultural significance of craft skills in the last few years and lacemaking in particular has provoked considerable debate and discussion within the visual arts. The medium of drawing is also under scrutiny as an area which has been significantly reconsidered by contemporary artists and which has consequently been reestablished as a powerfully autonomous fine

art medium. My work has been created in response to these debates, but has also acted as a stimulus for dialogue about both drawing and craft by providing a new visual language through which to examine both subjects.

I want my drawings to highlight the demise of the hand-made lace industry, the enduring innovation of machine-made lace and to increase the understanding of how these two industries are documented and archived by our public museums. Most importantly by using a low-tech hand-made process, such as drawing, I want to promote discussion about the loss of craft skills in a digital age and to provide audiences with a visual understanding of the impact of these changes.

The drawing process that I use, although time-consuming, is intensely meditative and this experience is passed onto the viewer who can engage with the process as well as the subject. The viewer is thus able to have an authentic and perhaps emotional encounter with the drawing in the same way that they would with the piece of lace. This would be less likely if the drawing were not created by hand.

The drawings have been shown alongside the real examples of lace that I have drawn and this encourages the viewer to take a closer look at the lace itself; and by understanding the relationship between the painstaking method of production of the drawings and the highly skilled and time-consuming production of the lace, to reconsider their perceptions of each. The majority of lace in museum collections is usually kept out of sight in storage and these drawings provide an opportunity to bring the lace into the open and to be seen by a broader public audience.

Can you tell us more about the themes you explore through your lace drawing?
Characterised by a close resemblance to real fabric, the highly detailed ink drawings of hand-made lace from the V&A, the Fashion Museum in Bath and Exeter Museum have explored the impact of the lacemaking industry on the social history of women. The deceptive simplicity of the detailed, repetitive mark-making of the drawings references the period before the industrial revolution, when hand-made textiles were part of everyday domestic life for women. As my work has progressed, the link between the items of lace that I choose to draw and the museum collections to which they belong has become more central.

More recently I have made drawings of machine-made lace from the collection at Nottingham Castle Museum for the Lace Works exhibition. The transition from hand-made to machine-made lace in these drawings

Lace Doily
2009, ink on paper, 44 x 40 cm.
Courtesy the artist.

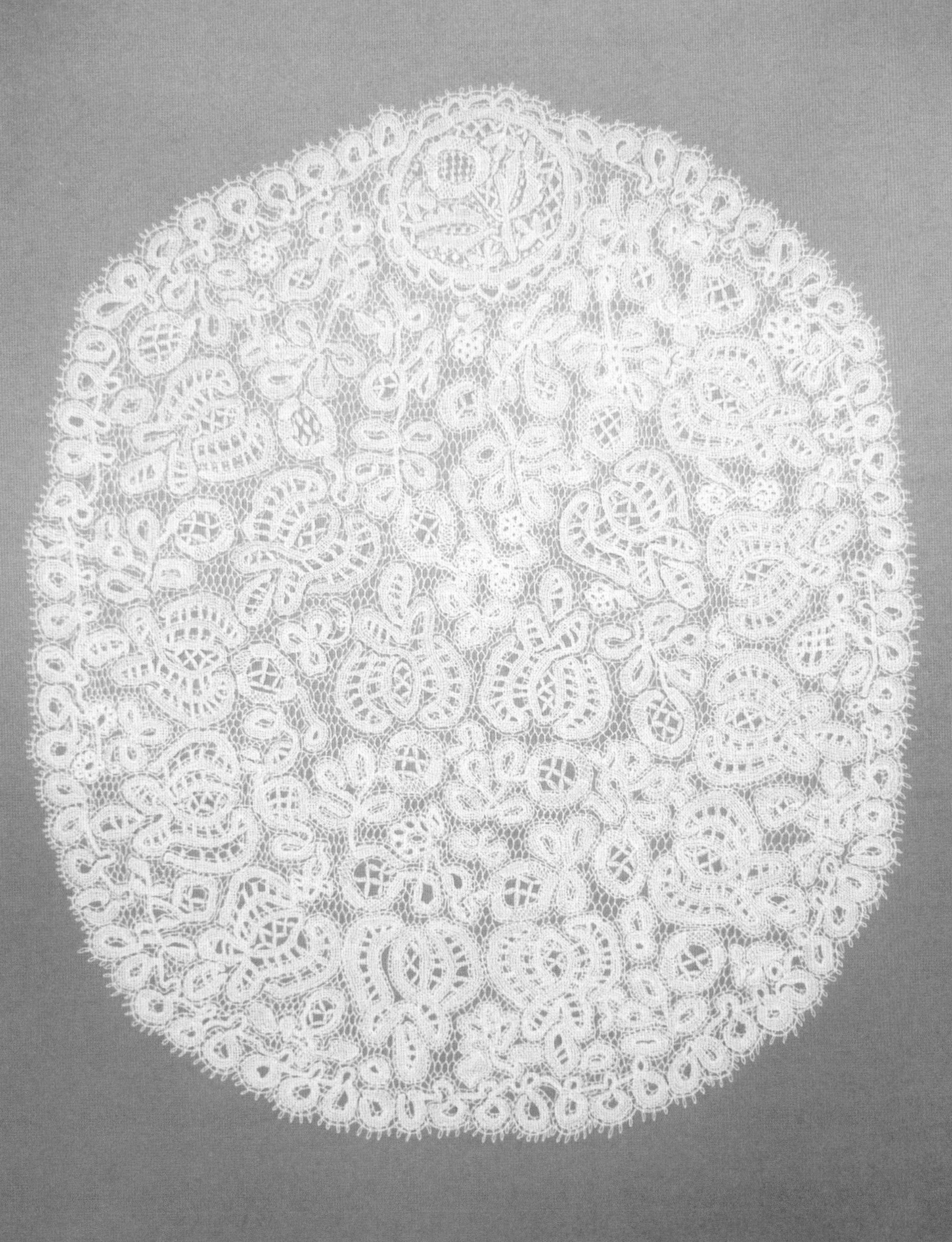

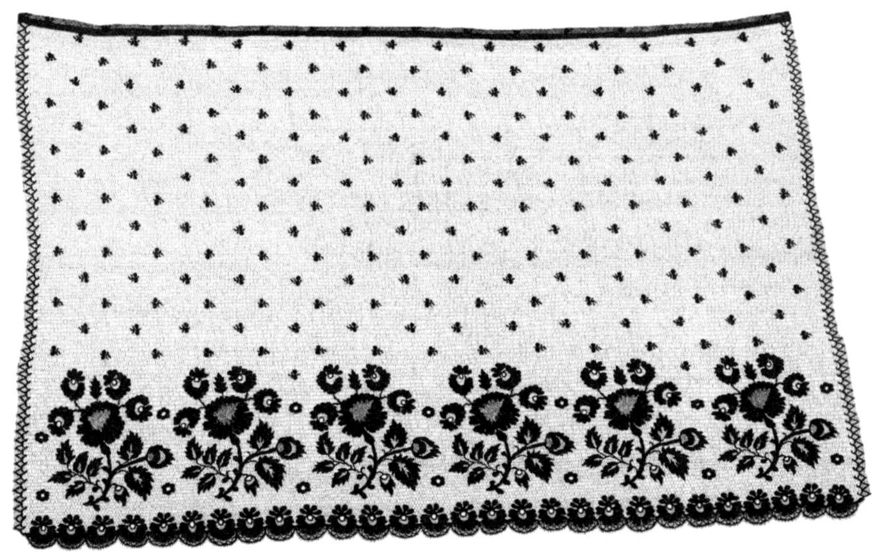

has uncovered some unexpected and intriguing contradictions and has generated further conversations and debate through which new themes have begun to emerge.

The panel of black Leaver's Lace from the Nottingham Castle Museum collection depicted in the drawing Nottingham Machine Lace is extremely fine and delicate but has been produced by a large, noisy machine and is in fact quite different from the hand-made lace it emulated in that it is more repetitive in technique and less complex in design. The inconsistencies between the two types of lace is further emphasised by the fact that the lace panel in the drawing has evidently been quite roughly cut from a bolt of fabric, the relative cheapness of the machine-made in comparison to the hand-made lace is thereby unmistakable.

Would you consider any other medium or fabric to express ideas in your work?

As well as lace, I have also drawn textiles such as whitework and embroidery and fabrics like muslin and lawn; some of the basic lace techniques resemble knitting and simple weaving which I have also drawn. I am very interested in contemporary woven textiles some of which are highly experimental and much less ordered than lace and I would like to experiment with translating these into drawing. However, there is still so much I want to do with lace that it may be a while before I move into other areas.

Charlotte Bronte's Shawl
2011, ink on paper,
62 x 100 cm.
Courtesy the artist.

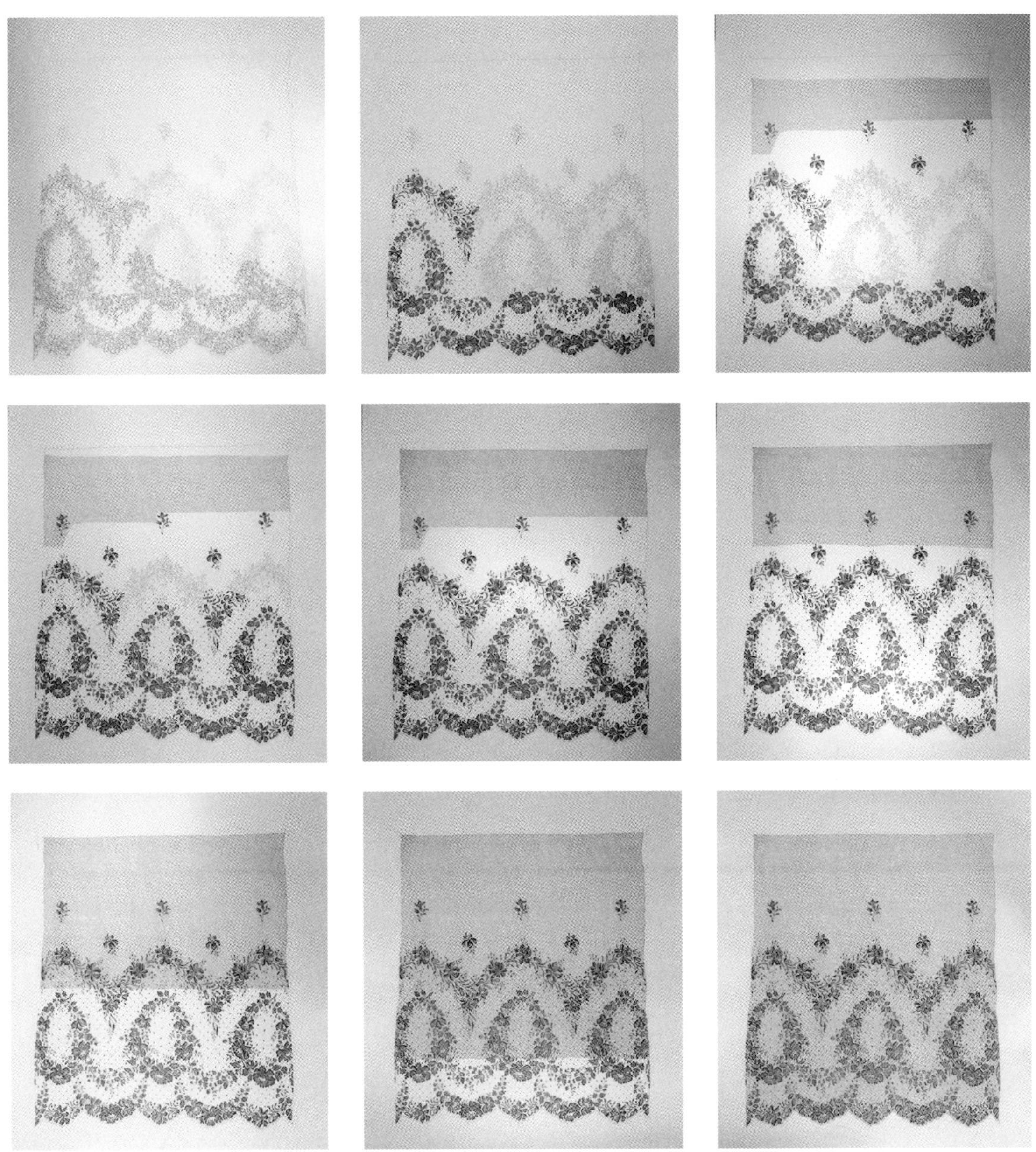

<u>Nottingham Machine Lace</u>
2012, progression of artwork, ink
on paper, 78 x 66 cm.
Courtesy the artist.

Thanks go to

For supporting the development of this publication:

Arts Council England.

Nottingham Trent University (NTU), in particular, Pro-Vice Chancellor Ann Priest.

Nottingham City Museums and Galleries (NCMG).

Dr Joy Buttress for her commitment, hard work and creative thinking to collate and resolve the publication.

To those who have contributed to the book, giving time generously and freely: Paul Simmons, Timorous Beasties, Sheila Mason, Judy Edgar, Matt Gill, Teresa Whitfield, Cecilia Heffer.

Dr Iryna Kuksa for proofreading.

For supporting the development of the season lace:here:now:

Research Fellow Joy Buttress for contributing to the organisation and direction of the season.

NTU Marketing Assistant: Sarah Connor for her incredible organisational skills.

NCMG for their help with preparing collection items for display: Judith Edgar, Victoria Hobbs, Haidee Jackson.

For all of those who contributed and participated in the events that formed lace:here:now:

Experience Nottinghamshire
Debbie Bryan—Nottinghamshire Craft Trail
Lesley Beale—Lakeside Arts Centre
Sue Pike, Helena Tomlin, Geoff Litherland—NTU
Edward Jarvis—Filmmaker
Sheila Mason—Historian
Peter Davidson—Storyteller
Madeleine Burt—Artist
Victoria Brown—Artist
Louise West—Artist
Tom Partridge—Graphic Designer
Broadway Cinema
Midland Archive of Central England (MACE)
Nottingham Industrial Museum
Framework Knitters Museum
Newstead Abbey
The Nottingham Festival of Words
Nottingham Contemporary
New College Nottingham
Warped event—Nicola Donovan—Artist.

For all of those who contributed and participated in the symposium Lace: heritage and contemporary practice:

Professor Julian Ellis
Teresa Whitfield
Danica Maier
Lucy Brown
Professor Lesley Millar
Paul Simmons.

Designed by Sylvia Ugga at Black Dog Publishing
Cover image: *Devil Damask Lace* www.timorousbeasties.com

Black Dog Publishing Limited
10a Acton Street, London WC1X 9NG
United Kingdom

Tel: +44 (0)20 7713 5097
Fax: +44 (0)20 7713 8682
info@blackdogonline.com
www.blackdogonline.com

British Library Cataloguing-in-Publication Data.
A CIP record for this book is available from the British Library.
ISBN 978 1 908966 36 0

Black Dog Publishing Limited, London, UK,
is an environmentally responsible company.
Lace:Here:Now is printed on sustainably sourced paper.

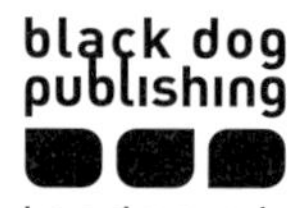

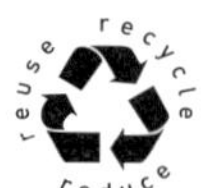

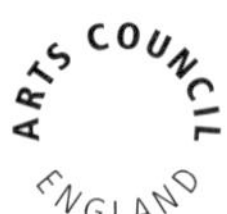

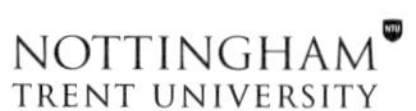

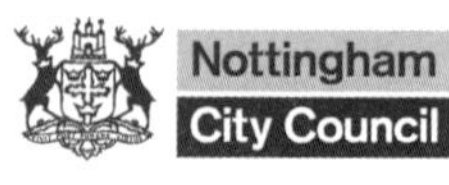